MORE PRAISE FOR *A Journal for Jordan*

"Gut-wrenching . . . Candy writes with the objective eye of a hard-line reporter yet manages to convey the complexities of the love between her and her fiancé as well as the deep loss she feels in his absence. It's impossible to imagine what her pain is like, but she does a beautiful job of allowing us to come close."
—*Washington Post*

"It's impossible not to be affected by her story."
—*Entertainment Weekly*

"Powerful . . . Not all great love stories are ignited by the lightning bolt of love at first glance; this humbler I'm-going-to-talk-myself-into-this-good-man version is believable and real. . . . *A Journal for Jordan* is impossible to read without a sense of bitter knowledge that this principled man fell at the behest of leaders less guided by honor. That is no trick O. Henry ending. It is a denouement full of suffering, worthy of Chekhov."
—MELISSA FAY GREENE, *New York Times*

"This tragic story of love and war reminds all Americans that we are fortunate to have people like Sergeant Charles King willing to die for our country. Dana Canedy bears witness to the enduring power of love, to Sergeant King's heroism, and to his unfailing devotion to his family and his men."
—CAROLINE KENNEDY

"Heartfelt . . . Canedy used her skills as a reporter to dig beneath the official story of King's death. . . . These investigative passages are gripping. . . . **King died a hero's death, but Canedy's embrace of life is a kind of heroism, too."**

—*Cleveland Plain Dealer*

"Canedy's memoir speaks to military families everywhere. . . . It speaks to their constant fear, anger, and confusion. . . . By openly and honestly revealing her side of their highly emotional story . . . she gives the project a greater significance, making it especially **relevant for and meaningful to countless others in similar situations."**

—*San Francisco Chronicle*

"Dana Canedy's moving memoir has captured my heart and won't let it go. **Courageous in its honesty and at times unsettling, it draws us deep into the soul of a woman in love, the pain of her loss, and the unpardonable theft of hopes and dreams, lives and futures stolen by war.** With an exquisite voice, Canedy recounts moments of intense emotion that haunt us long after savoring the last lines. I didn't want it to end."

—SUSAN L. TAYLOR, editor in chief emeritus, *Essence*

"Dana Canedy's talent at evoking character makes the account of King's life and death not simply a story about the injustice of war but a project in resurrection."

—DANIELLE TRUSSONI, *New York Times Book Review*

A Journal for Jordan

A STORY OF LOVE AND HONOR

DANA CANEDY

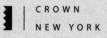

CROWN
NEW YORK

Published in the United States by Crown, an imprint of Random House,
a division of Penguin Random House LLC, New York.

CROWN and the Crown colophon are registered trademarks
of Penguin Random House LLC.

Originally published in hardcover in the United States by Crown,
an imprint of Random House, a division of Penguin Random House LLC,
New York, in 2008. Subsequently published in trade paperback in the
United States by Three Rivers Press, an imprint of the Crown Publishing
Group, a division of Penguin Random House LLC, New York, in 2009.

Photograph insert credits: page 6: Ozier Muhammad/*New York Times*;
page 8: Charles M. King; all other photographs are courtesy of the author.

Library of Congress Cataloging-in-Publication Data
King, Charles Monroe, d. 2006
A journal for Jordan / Charles Monroe King.
p. cm.
1. King, Charles Monroe, d. 2006. 2. Iraq War, 2003—Personal narra-
tives, American. 3. Soldiers—United States—Correspondence.
I. Canedy, Dana. II. Title.
DS79.76.K545 2008 956.7044'3—dc22 2008034135

ISBN 978-0-593-44293-7
Ebook ISBN 978-0-307-44971-9

Printed in the United States of America on acid-free paper

crownpublishing.com

2 4 6 8 9 7 5 3 1

Design by Lauren Dong

Motion Picture Artwork © 2021 CTMG. All Rights Reserved.

For Charles and Jordan,

keepers of my heart

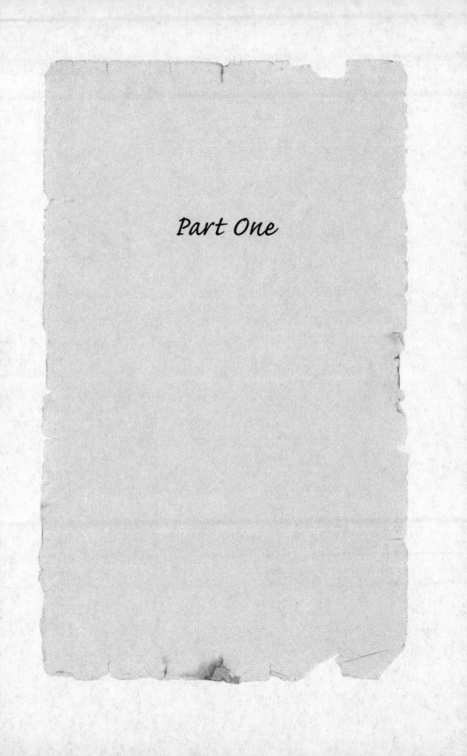

Part One

One

Dear Jordan,

If you are reading this book, it means that we got through the sorrowful years, somehow, and that you are old enough to understand all that I am about to tell you.

You are just ten months old now, but I am writing this for the young man you will be. By then, you will know that your father was a highly decorated soldier who was killed in combat in October 2006, when a bomb exploded beneath his armored vehicle in Iraq. You were six months old.

You will know that he left a journal for you, more than two hundred pages long, which he handwrote in neat block letters in that hot, terrifying place. What I want to tell you is how the journal came to be and what it leaves unsaid about your father and our abiding love.

Before he kissed my swollen stomach and left for the war in December 2005, your father, U.S. Army First Sergeant Charles Monroe King, had been preparing for the promise of your new life and for the possible end of his own. Even before he boarded that plane headed for danger, I worried that he would be killed. So I gave him a journal. I hoped he would write a few messages, perhaps some words of encouragement to you, though you were not yet born, in case he died before you knew each other.

We did a lot to prepare for the possibility that your father would miss out on your life, including finding out if you were a boy or a girl before he left; he was thrilled to have an image of you in his mind and kept your sonogram pictures in a pocket in his uniform the whole time he was in Iraq.

And then there was the journal. Writing it would be a way for your dad to help guide you through life if he did not make it home to us. He wanted you to know to pick up the check on a date, to take plenty of pictures on vacations, to have a strong work ethic, and to pay your bills on time. He wanted to tell you how to deal with disappointment, to understand the difference between love and lust, to remember to get on your knees and pray every day. Most of all, he wanted you to know how much he loved us.

So, late into the night in Iraq, after he had completed dangerous and often deadly missions, your dad returned hungry and exhausted to the relative calm of his room and wrote to you before he slept. His grammar was not perfect and his handwriting at times suggested that he was tired or rushed. But he put so much thought into the beautiful messages he wrote, things like:

> *Be humble about your accomplishments, work harder than the man next to you, it is all right for boys to cry. Sometimes crying can release a lot of pain and stress. Never be ashamed to cry. It has nothing to do with your manhood.*

Your father mailed the journal to me in July 2006, shortly after one of his young soldiers was killed in an explosion eerily similar to the one that would claim his own life. He was so shaken after pulling the young man's body, piece by piece, out of a bombed tank that he sent the journal to me, unfinished. He had more to say, but that would have to wait until he came home on a two-week leave to meet you, six weeks before he died.

I read the journal in the calm of night on the day it arrived, with you sleeping next to me, and fell in love with my gentle warrior all over again. He was the most honorable man I have ever known, and the most complex. I do not want to portray your dad as a saint whose example you could never live up to. He was not. He was gentle, benevolent, and loyal, but he could also be moody, stubborn, and withholding. He would brood for days over a perceived slight, like the time I spent my birthday with my sisters and girlfriends instead of with him. He put his military service ahead of his family.

I also want you to understand me—an imperfect woman who deeply loved her man but struggled during our long courtship to accept him as he was. We were together for the better part of a decade, half of which he spent waiting for me to fall in love with him. Truth be told, every girl has an image of the man with whom she will walk down the aisle one day, and he was not the groom I had imagined. He was excruciatingly introverted, a procrastinator, and got his news, God forgive him, from television instead of the *New York Times*, where I have worked as a journalist for more than eleven years.

I am loquacious, assertive, and impatient, which mostly amused your father but sometimes annoyed him. I am also obstinate and impulsive. My weight fluctuates when I am stressed. I curse in traffic.

I had a demanding career as a reporter when I met your father, while he was away for months at a time in the wilderness, training young men for battle. A former drill sergeant, he had a strong sense of duty. He was so devoted to his troops, many just out of high school, that he bailed them out of jail, taught them to balance their checkbooks, and even advised them about birth control. I learned to live with his long silences and ambivalence toward newspapers. But I struggled to understand what motivated the man who had for so long dreamed of your birth but chose to miss it because he believed his soldiers needed him more. He refused to take his leave from Iraq until all 105 of his men had gone home first.

Your father was bound to the military not only by a sense of duty, but because it had expanded his world. The soldiers he trained, and trained with, came from coal mining towns in West Virginia, the Bronx in New York City, seaside villages in Puerto Rico. He met former surfers, men who shared his love for the Bible, and women he revered for excelling in a male-dominated institution. He traveled through Europe while stationed in Germany. He practiced his Spanish while working with Cuban refugees at Guantanamo Bay. He wrote in the journal:

> *Enlisting in the army was one of the best decisions I had ever made in my life. God blessed me above all I could imagine. Like anything, you have some challenging days, but when I look back I have no regrets. The army even recognized my artistic abilities. I also met a lot of great people. It's been an awesome experience. Thanks, God.*

But those were peacetime experiences. The military had also introduced Charles to killing and death. The sight of blood gave him flashbacks. Chemical sprays he received during the First Gulf War left permanent splotches on his arms. For years he was haunted by images of combat, unable to speak about them even to me.

During his final tour of duty, he experienced loss of the worst kind. His goal was to bring every one of his men home alive; he even made that promise to many of their wives. It was a vow he could not keep. Still, he never questioned the rightness of a single mission. For Charles, the war was not about "weapons of mass destruction" or an "axis of evil"; I never heard him speak those words. It was about leading the soldiers he had trained by example, about honor and dignity, and about protecting a country he loved from enemies real or imagined.

I am proud of your dad's honor and dignity—even of the way he died. Son, all of us will leave this world, but so few die a hero's death.

Still, the would-be wife and new mother in me are angry at times that he left us so early, at the age of forty-eight. Was it heroic or foolish that he volunteered for the mission that killed him?

As the daughter of an army veteran, I grew up on or near military bases and after I left for college wanted no more of that life. So for years I resisted getting deeply involved with your father, and much of our long-distance romance involved him chasing me and me pushing him away. We dated other people at times, me out of a fear of committing to your father, him out of frustration with my dithering. Ultimately, it was his steadiness, his character, and his sureness about who he was and what he stood for that won me over, something you will get to know by reading the journal.

Listen to your first thought. You will figure this out on your own. Never second-guess yourself. When your heart is in the right place, always go with your first thought. Work hard at things and follow your instinct. Since you were born, you have always been alert. That means you will be very perceptive about things. Believe God and trust yourself. Keep the faith, Jordan. You will be fine.

Your dad wanted so badly for you to know him that he revealed himself in the journal in a way he rarely did in person. He told you things about himself that I never knew. He wrote that he wanted to see the Great Wall of China and to take guitar lessons. He went into detail about his love of art, his religious faith, and his childhood in Cleveland. I laughed as I pictured my soldier wearing stack-heeled shoes and bell-bottom pants in junior high school.

My favorite stack-heeled shoes were bought from a shoe store called Thom McCann. They were black patent leather with a suede heel. Now Grandma King would always say stack-heeled shoes were no good for your back. I guess I had to learn the hard way. I was walking downtown and glanced over at my reflection in a department store window. I was walking hunched like an old man. I had to throw them away.

Until I read the journal I did not know that your father sang in the youth choir at his multicultural Methodist church, was a life-long Cleveland Browns fan, and had his first kiss in the eighth grade with a girl named Denise.

> *I walked her home after school and she thanked me by giving me a kiss. I was a little taken back by it. Being in the eighth grade, it was a big step for me. All the girls were always smiling at me and joking around.*
>
> *I remember buying a brand-new baseball jacket. I took it to school and let all the girls sign it and put their phone numbers on it. I had the jacket in my room and Grandma King grabbed it thinking it was dirty and washed it. I rushed home from school, anxious to read my jacket, when I saw Grandma King hanging up my clean jacket. Grandma laughed. I was on my knees crying.*

Your dad was an extraordinarily disciplined man. He believed that sweating on a five-mile run was the best way to shake a cold. He picked the skin off chicken, would not drink more than one or two beers in a night, and did not allow himself to binge on the pastries he loved because he so closely watched his diet.

Despite his regimented manner, there was so much depth to your father's character. He had a mind for war strategy but drew angels bowed in prayer. He spent hours sculpting a taut body, even starting his days in Iraq in a gym at 5 a.m., but he loved my more-than-ample curves and had the softest skin I have ever touched. He gave away copies of his art to soldiers he respected but would shout his throat raw when they made mistakes in training that could cost them their lives in combat. "When he yelled, you moved," one of the officers he served with said in a eulogy at his funeral. "Because he only yelled when there was good reason."

This tough guy was the same man who liked to feed me champagne, popcorn, and chocolate in bed. The man who loved you so dearly that during the two weeks he had with you that August—the only two weeks—he barely slept. He preferred to spend that too-brief time dancing around with you in his arms, taking you to the bookstore for story time, and simply watching you sleep. He rarely discussed his personal life at work, but after he died his soldiers said that they knew that when he was "working" in his office, he was often gazing at pictures of us.

His imposing presence was really a mask for his shyness. Simple things brought him pleasure: drawing pictures of me, starting the day in prayer, summer rainstorms.

Sometimes you get lucky and catch a rainbow.

I never knew the fierce warrior who led those troops, and I was sometimes a mystery to him, too. He thought I talked things to death. He read my newspaper stories if I asked him to, but he had no concept of how I could report and write about something momentous, a murder trial or a space shuttle explosion, in an afternoon. He also never understood how I could splurge on a diamond tennis bracelet but go to three stores to find the best price on mustard. He thought I sometimes expected too much of him, which perhaps I did.

Still, we were in love. By the time he received his orders for Iraq in December 2004, we were finally ready to be a family. We decided to have you. At forty years old, I got pregnant in one passionate weekend when your father was on a break from training.

Then, in the dusk of an early spring day nearly four months after he left for Iraq, I lay in a hospital bed giving birth to you, wracked by a pain so intense I did not think my body could endure it. I could not know that only six months later I would fall to the floor screaming from a pain more wrenching than childbirth, when I learned that your father had been killed. That night I reached for your journal, and I have read it a hundred times since. I find new insights every time.

Your father had waited a long time for a son and wanted to be the kind of father you could admire. He had tried to be a good father to Christina, his daughter from a marriage that had ended in divorce, and it had always pained him that he didn't spend more time with her.

> *To be a good father I think you have to be a good provider. That's not all. You should be a good communicator who has open views, accepts changing times. Be around for significant events. Be there to encourage you in whatever endeavors you desire. A good father always makes himself available.*

Besides keeping the journal, Charles also wrote more than a dozen love letters to me while he was at war, and I want to share some of them with you as well. He wrote about the dangers he was facing and the things he missed: time to draw, home-cooked meals, the feel of my skin. And he wrote longingly about you:

> *I'm anxious to see you and Jordan. I remember our*
> *visit when you were hoping for his conception. Dreams*
> *come true. Love, Charles.*

I still find myself talking about your dad in the present tense; my mind has not yet recalibrated itself. I take comfort in knowing that we left nothing unsaid and treasure mementos like the set of dog tags he left on my nightstand when he first left for the war. The cold aluminum on my chest and the clink of the tags make me feel as though he is making his presence known.

I miss everything about your father and am so afraid I will forget the details that only I noticed: the way his ears turned red when I kissed them, the way he tilted his head back when he laughed, the scar on his right knee that I still trace in my mind.

I miss the way he held you.

I pray that by the time you read this book a scar will have formed over the gash in my heart. But your father has only been gone four months now and I am still hurting and scared and sometimes even angry at him for dying. Most of all, I am thankful that you are too young to feel this agony, so raw that even breathing hurts.

If I find the strength to be the mother I hope to be in the years ahead, you will savor life rather than simply survive it. You will laugh loud and often. You will see the world and contribute to it. If so, I will not be able to claim all the credit for shaping such a fine young man. Your father, though he left us before you knew him, will have helped.

The journal is now tucked away, and I have no answer when people ask me when I will show it to you.

Some nights, as I stand over your crib watching you sleep, I am overcome with the pain of losing your dad. Yet even then, I know that the war did not steal him from us entirely. It could not steal that precious journal, written so lovingly, from my soldier to my son.

Two

Dear Jordan,

The first time I saw Charles Monroe King, he was standing in the living room of the gray stone ranch house where I grew up on a cul-de-sac in Radcliff, Kentucky, an outpost of Fort Knox army base. It was Father's Day weekend, 1998, and I was visiting my dad out of obligation as much as affection. My father, a former drill sergeant who in his day looked like a shorter version of Muhammad Ali, had warned me since I was a teenager that I would one day regret not being a more dutiful daughter. "You aren't going to appreciate me until I'm dead and gone," he would say.

So I tried, honestly I did, to be the girl he thought I should be. The trouble was, it meant almost complete obedience. For a time growing up we kids weren't allowed to use the dishwasher because he felt it encouraged laziness. Some evenings he would find smudges on drinking glasses, a speck of food in a bowl, or water spots on a fork. "Look at these dishes. They aren't clean," he would bark at us if he didn't like what he saw. It was understood that we had to rewash them. Being a good girl also meant not challenging his views, even when he thundered about being the breadwinner who made our lives possible and belittled my mother's contributions. It meant pretending along with her not to notice when he took my younger brother and three sisters to visit his lover in the town's public housing development. My father expected us to follow his commands without hesitation, and we seldom risked crossing him.

I was the oldest child and headstrong, though. In my bravest moments, I was the one—the only one, my mother included—who dared stand up to him. It was always with great trepidation, but it became part of my role in our family. One time during my freshman year in college, I was home for the weekend and my dad wanted to drive my car—to visit his mistress, I knew. I had worked all summer serving burgers at a fast-food restaurant to pay for the used silver Datsun 260Z and did not want him to take it. So when he headed out of the dining room toward the front door with my keys, I followed him.

"You are *not* driving my car to visit that woman," I said, my legs shaking but not buckling.

He threw the keys on the floor, told me I was disrespectful, and brushed past me. It was not until the door slammed behind him and I heard him start the engine of his aging blue van that I exhaled and picked up my keys.

For me, what growing up as one of T.J. and Penny Canedy's five children mostly meant was marking the years, then the months, and finally the days until I graduated from high school and could leave for good. But for good never came. I always joked that my family put the funk in dysfunction, but still we loved one another. I admired my father's physical strength (my siblings and I took turns sitting on his back when he did push ups) and his work ethic. He left the house before dawn to put his trainees through their drills. He drove a cab at night and dished popcorn at a movie theater on weekends. (We looked forward to digging in to the commercial-size trash bags full of leftover popcorn he would bring home.)

I also learned from him that a father never ate all of the food on his plate; he saved some for whichever child might still be hungry after the pot of chili or butter beans ran out.

Above all, I learned about discipline from my father, for he could be as strict with himself as he was with us. When I was fourteen, he quit drinking and smoking cigarettes cold turkey. It was a conversation with my sister Kim that sparked it. He had always called her a "junk-food junkie" because she ate so much candy. "If you stop eating candy for a week, I'll stop smoking," he told her one day, stowing his Salem Menthols in a drawer. Not long after that, he realized that he probably ought to stop drinking, too. From that day forward, there would be no more Pabst Blue Ribbon or Smirnoff in the house. And my sister stopped eating sweets.

My mother was a tall, slim woman with the biggest brown eyes I had ever seen, and the smoothest maple-brown skin. She always looked ten years younger than her age, and more than one of my boyfriends remarked on how "fine" my older sister was. She had a youthful spirit, too, and loved to dance—fingers popping and hips gyrating—to anything soulful when she was not suffering from bouts of depression that silenced her laugh and left her unable to comb her hair.

Even on her worst days, my mother contributed more to our family than my father acknowledged. She made the best Halloween costumes—a hobo from sheets, a robot from an appliance box. When we found some abandoned baby rabbits in our backyard, she helped us try to raise them. I loved the feel of her hands rubbing Vicks on my chest when I was home from school with the flu. I savored having her all to myself.

But after she nursed me back to health, time alone with my mother would be elusive. She was not comfortable showing affection, perhaps because, as a child, she had been sexually abused by several relatives. All I knew was that she rarely held or kissed me, even when I got my heart broken.

My mom was a PTA president and led a Girl Scout troop, but she also rarely talked to me about drugs or sex or dating and had no interest in fashion and makeup. Trying to find my way alone caused embarrassing moments in high school. How was I to know that bright orange bell-bottoms were out of style and frosted blue was not the best shade of eye shadow for a brown-eyed black girl?

It was not just her attention I craved. It was the physical closeness. I do not remember her ever reading me a bedtime story. At times my mother's ways could be cruel and confusing. After my sister Lynnette took my father's side in an argument between my parents, my mother punished her by making her go to school with her hair unkempt. "Let your father comb it," my mother said to her, knowing he had already left for work. My sister was only six or seven.

When I was a teen and given to being obstinate, my mother would regularly admonish me that "you'll need me before I need you!" The words hurt as much as any spanking, and I have spent much of my life determined never to be needy.

My siblings and I learned to provide whatever nurturing our parents could not. We huddled the night my father broke his thumb punching our mother in the chest. After one of us got a "belt whipping," another would sneak into the bedroom with a washcloth full of ice to ease the sting, or a handful of toilet paper to dab at tears. The ice was especially soothing when one of us—usually me—tried not to cry during one of those whippings. Such behavior was considered an act of defiance that would be met by harsher lashes until we wailed.

Of course my siblings and I fought over whose turn it was to clean up the yard after Major, our Doberman pinscher, or which one of us was entitled to the last slice of mom's pineapple upside-down cake. We never stayed mad long, though. We made Barbie houses out of shoeboxes, decorated the cut-out windows with curtains made from scraps of fabric, and glued together Popsicle sticks to make furniture. My brother occasionally joined in with his G.I. Joes but was more apt to pull pranks. Once he caught a cricket and kept it in a box to use to torment me. He sneaked it under my bedroom door, and I screamed and gave him a quarter to remove it. The next day he did the same thing. At the end of the week he had a lot of quarters. His scheme only ended when our mother decided he had fooled me out of enough of my babysitting money.

We had our idiosyncrasies, we Canedys, but our family remained intact, and, eventually, when I was about twelve, we made it from the army base to Radcliff. My parents had both grown up poor in inner-city Indianapolis, met when she was seventeen and he was twenty, and married less than a year later. They dreamed of one day living in a newly constructed house with a yard and enough basement space for a family room. The house they finally saved enough money to buy was on a quiet middle-class street with one Asian, three black, and four white families. While it was understood among the neighbors that subjects like politics and race were not to be brought up, all the children on the circle played together, and the parents made easy conversation about the weather or the lushness of their chemically treated lawns.

Because of his climb up to a middle-class life, my father would admonish me not to forget where I came from or who had made possible whatever success I attained. It was that admonition that kept pulling me back to the house in Radcliff long after I had left, seeking a career as a writer. I was the first child on either side of our family to attend college and felt guilty when my father would scoff, "You act like you pulled yourself up by your bootie straps."

And so, on Father's Day 1998, when I was thirty-three, I went home once again in hopes of rewriting the role my father had cast me in, the ungrateful child who would not appreciate him until he was "dead and gone."

It was early Saturday afternoon and I had just arrived from the hotel where I was staying. When I walked into the living room a gorgeous man was standing there, holding a framed picture. I could not help but stare. I do not quite remember what I noticed first. The soft light brown eyes outlined by long black lashes? The skin the color of smooth caramel? The thick black mustache flecked with gray? I could see the outline of his beautiful body, even hidden underneath an oversize, faded T-shirt and baggy jeans cinched tight with a belt. He had swollen biceps and a hulking chest and shoulder muscles. His waist was so tiny it seemed out of proportion. Even the muscles in his hands bulged.

The combination of his sculpted body and gentle face made the spot behind my navel flutter the way it always does when I crave a man. But it wasn't just that. It was the way he lowered his head, too shy to look directly at me. I wondered how a man blessed with so much beauty could possibly be bashful.

"Well, hello," I said, walking into the room and extending my hand. "I'm Dana."

"Hi, I'm Charles," he said, nodding in my direction and briefly taking my hand.

I was close enough now to see the picture he was holding. It was a black-and-white collage of images of my father as a drill sergeant, created with thousands of tiny dots of ink. It must have taken hours of patient, exacting work. There my father was, smiling proudly near a tank and, in another image, carrying a company flag and leading his troops to their graduation ceremony. I had never seen anything like it.

Charles was holding it with some measure of pride, so I asked whether he had drawn it.

"Yes," he said, lowering his eyes. He seemed embarrassed.

"That's incredible," I said.

"Thank you."

I admired the portrait as Charles stood there in silence, smiling, until a few minutes later when my mother walked in. It turned out that it was a gift to my father, and she had been looking for the right place to hang it.

After excusing myself to get a glass of water, I found my father in the kitchen.

"Dad, who is that guy?" I whispered.

"Oh, that's Charles," my father said. "Nice looking, isn't he?"

I took a long drink of water and waited, self-conscious, for my father to tell me more. He said Charles was stationed at Fort Knox and that he was an artist who specialized in pointillist portraits in ink like the one I had just seen. He also used pencils, charcoal, and watercolors. Charles drew portraits of black tankers from World War II, Bedouins, cowboys, and African mothers in native dress holding their children.

"We met him on post when he was showing his art at an exhibit," my father said. "Nice man. Talented, too."

"Is he single?"

"Yes, but—"

He could not finish because suddenly there was Charles to say that he was leaving. There was no time to waste; I needed a way to get his attention before one of my single sisters noticed him. We had a rule that any man was fair game until one of us claimed him.

I hastily announced that I had checked into a hotel near Fort Knox, a place I often stayed when I visited to give myself a bit of solitude at the end of emotionally charged days. "Would you mind giving me a ride if you're going that way?" I asked Charles.

"No problem," he said. Charles followed me out the front door, past the giant oak tree and down the pebble driveway to his black 1989 Mustang. He stole glances at me as we drove in silence and I searched for something to say. Not only did he not speak, he didn't even have the radio on. For someone like me, who loves to talk and fire off questions—and does that for a living—it was excruciating. Charles seemed the opposite of the gregarious alpha men who have always stopped me cold. He had an eagle feather hanging from a cord on the rearview mirror. (Was it a good luck talisman? I never did find out.) He drove agonizingly slowly, and I could feel the tension rising in my head and legs. I wanted to press on the floorboard with my foot, as if that would make us go faster. Who actually drove forty-five in a forty-five-miles-per-hour speed zone—with both hands on the wheel?

I was born a month premature, which is to say I have always been in a hurry. What I wanted was an instant connection with this polite artist-soldier who was clearly used to taking his time. He had gotten my attention without words, but for all I knew he had a type, too, and it might not be a curvy, career-driven woman whose last trip to the gym was for a massage. I have turned a head or two with my long, honey-colored legs and almond-shaped eyes, but most of the men who have been attracted to me have been drawn to my smile, exuberance, and wit, not my well-padded abs. I had no idea whether Charles was available or interested.

"Do you have time to sit with me by the pool for a little while?" I asked as we pulled into the hotel parking lot.

"Sure, I guess," he said, sounding surprised.

He walked around to open my door, but I was already halfway out of the car; I made a mental note to stay put if there was a next time. He followed me through the hotel lobby, stopping at a vending machine to buy sodas. I opened the glass door leading to the indoor pool, and the humidity and chlorine hit me in the face. I took off my shoes and sat with my legs dangling in the pool. A group of children splashed in the shallow end. Charles knelt next to me with his running shoes still laced up, watching as I wiggled my toes in the water and hummed. He seemed amused by my spontaneity. I could have sat there all afternoon except that water began to soak through my pants, so I moved to a pair of plastic chairs and Charles followed along.

I asked him how well he knew my parents, and he told me they were like family to him. "I've been going through a lot," he said.

"I'm sorry. What's been going on?"

He was quiet for a long while and then came out with it: he was divorcing his wife. This was the most painful period of his life, he said. He also said that my father had been a good listener and my mother had invited him over on weekends for her barbequed ribs. "They've really been there for me. I'm so grateful."

After watching my parents hurt each other so often, I had spent much of my adult life protecting my heart and not trusting most men. That my mother and father should have anything to offer a person in a crumbling relationship struck me as laughable.

"That's nice," I said, keeping a straight face.

Part of my job as a journalist is to take stock of people quickly, and I somehow knew that Charles was not the kind of man who would open up to a stranger without prodding. So I asked where he was from.

Cleveland, and he was forty-one, with a younger sister. His parents were churchgoing folks from Alabama, a nutritionist and a nurse. In the journal he would later write:

> *I was born and raised in Cleveland. It was not always easy growing up in Cleveland, but it made me tough and I learned to survive around people who were a bad influence.*
>
> *I learned that no matter where you grow up, whether rich or poor, you always have choices to do the right thing or the wrong thing. Nobody twists your arm. If they don't like your decision, you stand up for yourself. It's your life, not theirs.*

Maybe he was nervous or had somewhere else to be. In any case, he stood up and abruptly said he would be on his way. He said he would stop by my parents' house in the morning to wish my dad a happy Father's Day and offered to pick me up at 9 a.m.

I did not tell him that I rarely got out of bed before noon on weekends and certainly not before I had read the front section of the *Times*. It was one of the benefits of being single and childless.

"Great," I lied. "I'll be ready."

I saw him off and then called one of my sisters to drive me back to my parents' house. I had not actually wanted to go back to the hotel, of course. But I had needed information about Charles. And now, according to the sisterhood code, I had the right of first refusal.

Charles intrigued me but, as I saw it, he had at least two obvious negatives. He was a military man like my father, and, worse, his friend. What girl wanted to be romantic with Daddy's buddy? The ride home in the morning, bleary though it might be, would provide an opportunity for more probing.

The former drill sergeant arrived precisely at 9 a.m. and called from the lobby. I was nowhere near ready. Would he mind waiting on the balcony of my room overlooking the pool? I asked. Was I sure I wanted him to come up? he asked, which made me smile. Having grown accustomed to big-city men who assumed that tickets to a play, even off-Broadway, entitled them to a personal performance after the curtain came down, I considered this refreshingly chivalrous.

Charles arrived wearing a better-fitting shirt, but his jeans still sagged. He was carrying two cups of coffee and handed me one. It was the opening I needed, and I took a chance and gave him a thank-you hug. He was not as surprised as I had expected him to be and leaned in to meet my embrace. I held him there a moment more and breathed in his scent—musky, sweet. He briefly took my hand on the way to the car, and I liked the way my fingers felt in his tight grip. I let him open my door, proud of myself for remembering.

We agreed to stop at a store so that I could buy a card for my father, and he drove—well within the speed limit—to a supermarket. As I watched Charles walk, soldier-straight, to the bakery for pastries, I thought about the promise I had made to myself years ago to stay away from military men.

I knew I was getting ahead of myself, but I was drawn to Charles, and that unnerved me. I had never wanted to pack up my home every few years to follow a man to yet another military base. Most of the military wives I had known growing up in the 1970s had little control in their relationships. The soldier's life came first, even when that required his wife to be a single parent for a year while he served a "hardship" tour of duty in Korea. If you were inclined to work outside the home, you had to be prepared to resign if your soldier was restationed. You had to believe him, or pretend to, when he told you that one of his troops needed him in the middle of the night.

There were rules for the children of military men, too. You did not fight too often with the ranking soldier's kids down the street. You got used to your father being gone for weeks in the field to train. You learned to sleep through the sounds of machine guns and tanks firing at night because you knew it was only a drill.

The thing I hated most about military living was the "quarters," as government family housing is called. For years we lived on Fischer Avenue at Fort Knox and those quarters reminded me of cages—rows of brick-and-wood units divided by too-thin walls, with yards not much larger than parking spaces. You could hear your neighbor's toilet flush. Everyone on the block knew if your parents were having an argument, which mine often were.

Once, our next-door neighbor came over and asked to borrow a roll of toilet paper. Nobody had much money, but even at ten or eleven I was embarrassed for her. Another night, my mother knocked on that neighbor's door in urgent need of her own favor. I had been throwing up and had a dangerously high fever, and my mother needed to borrow a car to take me to the emergency room. (My father had come home hours earlier, unlaced his combat boots, changed out of his uniform, and driven off for the night.)

We were at the hospital until well after midnight, and I still remember lying on the backseat of our neighbor's car, weak and tired, after we left. I could tell we had taken a detour on the way home and lifted my head to see where we were. My mother was driving around the parking lot of a nightclub on the base, a place where countless soldiers had found and lost wives. I knew she was looking for our car. It was not there. I knew what that meant, too.

I am sure there were military wives who had good jobs and stable marriages, but I did not know any.

Being an army brat was not entirely bad. We played kickball with the other brats on the block until the streetlights came on. On hot days, when school was out, we aimed water hoses at one another. But I never got used to playmates packing up and leaving when their fathers got orders to report to Georgia or Germany. Within a month, there would be a new brat or two moving into the unit to replace the kid who had promised to call or write but never did.

No, life with a military man was not for me, and yet there I was, standing next to one in a checkout line and thinking that his gentleness and modesty affected me in a way that few people had in my life. Years later, when I read the journal, I learned that he felt the same, although he phrased it with his usual gentlemanly simplicity:

> *The first time we really spoke to each other I was going through a lot in my life. I felt very comfortable with her and was anxious to see her again.*

At the time I could tell that Charles was curious about me, amused even. He looked at me as though he had never seen someone say so much without taking a breath.

"So do you want to go somewhere for breakfast?" Charles asked when we were back in his car. He had already eaten a pastry. I smiled broadly. He was interested!

At a diner we ordered pancakes, and Charles bowed his head to pray before he ate. I was already chewing. I stopped and set down my fork. I prayed over my meals, too, when I remembered.

The sunlight streamed into our booth and we lingered long after we were full and our coffee had cooled. I braved the topic of his marriage.

Charles spoke vaguely of heartache so intense that he had sought medical treatment for what he thought at first was a heart attack but turned out to be anxiety. He had not been sleeping well, was lonely and worried about how to explain the unraveling of a family to an eight-and-a-half-year-old daughter who adored both of her parents.

"All I ever wanted was a family," he said.

I told him that I could relate to his pain. Not long before, I had broken up with a boyfriend who immediately fell in love with a woman who looked like a supermodel and had a Harvard MBA.

"Who gets all that?" I asked. "You either get the model or the Harvard MBA, not both!"

I didn't know then that Charles's wife, Cecilia King, was stunning, too—tall and spaghetti-thin, with skin the color of cocoa beans, brown doe eyes, and round cheekbones the size of walnuts. Charles had fallen for her the moment they met, before he joined the military, when they were both doing catering work in a hotel banquet hall in Mobile, Alabama. Their daughter, Christina, had her mother's good looks and her father's tenderness. He seemed lost without them, grateful to have someone to sit across a table from at breakfast.

There was a silence. The waitress had cleared our table and stopped asking if we wanted more coffee, but we did not move.

"So what made you join the army?" I asked.

Charles said he was drawn to military service because of the discipline, the travel, and the mental and physical challenges. He had been in the army for nearly eleven years and planned to serve at least twenty before he retired to teach and pursue his art.

I learned he was a sergeant first class who helped run a platoon. He taught soldiers military doctrine and actually enjoyed leading them on uphill hikes carrying twenty pounds of equipment in the summer heat.

This was the same man who could barely look at me. The man, I would later learn, who took a sketch pad to Iraq during the First Gulf War and, between missions, sat on the hood of his tank drawing the local children.

Charles finally worked in a few questions of his own. What was it like, he asked, to live in New York City?

I told him that it was the opposite of Radcliff in nearly every conceivable way. McDonald's delivered Big Macs. There were day care centers for dogs. I probably walked three miles a day in New York, but in Radcliff I drove around the supermarket parking lot for ten minutes, looking for the spot nearest to the entrance. There was nothing like the dim sum in Chinatown or Rockefeller Center at Christmastime.

"If you love Monet," I said, "maybe I can show you the real thing."

Charles had mentioned that he was moving to Fort Riley, Kansas, in a few months, to start a new assignment. He was a newly single man whose heart was still bruised. I sipped the last of my cold coffee and wondered whether I would ever see him again.

Three

Dear Jordan,

If my family was boisterous and chaotic, your father's was hushed and polite. We settled our disputes with family summits, arguments, and the occasional shoving match. In the King household, whatever might cause a disturbance—resentments, money troubles, strong emotion of any kind—was suppressed. Your father's parents were determined to live peacefully and properly in a world that was increasingly turbulent.

Your grandfather Charlie—a towering disciplinarian who before you had even reached your first birthday said I should do my best to teach you to be quiet—took pride in having dutiful children. Your grandmother Gladys—a prim, mild-mannered woman who even as you were learning to use a sippy cup sent me a china demitasse with instructions to demonstrate how you should hold it—cared deeply about decorum.

"We never really liked a lot of conflict and so we just tried to make peace," she explained recently. "Maybe we went to the extreme, I don't know."

They lived in a modest one-story white house with sea foam green shutters in the working-class neighborhood of Lee-Harvard in Cleveland and both worked at the Veterans Administration hospital in Brecksville, Ohio, for close to thirty years. They spent their lives trying to turn the pain of how they had each grown up into something that would help others—although I do not know how much they were conscious of that. Mr. King had gone hungry for much of his childhood; now he worked as a dietitian, planning meals for vets who were injured or ill. Healthy eating became his lifelong obsession. Because your grandmother, a nurse, worked the 4 to 12 a.m. shift to be home during the day, it fell to your grandfather to feed your father and his sister. If he got home late, he would wake them for supper—something they were none too happy about.

"My dad was adamant about us eating three meals a day," your aunt Gail recalled.

It is typical of your father that he wrote less about his frustration with his parents' strict ways or with middle-of-the-night meals, and more about his father's resolve.

> *Dad grew up so poor that when he was a boy he remembered going to bed with his stomach growling. He made a promise that his kids would never go to sleep hungry.*

Charles Monroe King made his way into the world on June 10, 1958, a screaming 6 lb., 7 oz. baby with wisps of fine black hair. His vociferous arrival in a Cleveland hospital after ten hours of labor offered no sign of the child he would be.

Charles—or "Chuck," as they called him—was shy and sensitive, traits he got from his mother. "A gentle soul" is how she once described her boy.

> *I am blessed with good qualities from both my*
> *parents. From my mother I got my quietness.*
> *She's the one that always tried to remain calm.*

Chuck was devoted to his mother. The former Gladys Freeman was the beautiful daughter of a farmer and a domestic from rural Newell, Alabama. She was light-skinned with hazel eyes and wavy auburn hair that she wore in a tight ponytail. She collected antique china and books about history and art. On weekends, she would take Chuck and his younger sister, Gail, to museums and department stores downtown.

> *I enjoyed going downtown on Saturdays with Mom.*
> *I guess that's why I enjoy going out with your*
> *mother to shop. Your grandmother would give me*
> *my allowance and I would spend all day trying to*
> *decide what I would do or buy with it. I would*
> *usually end up with a model car. I loved to go*
> *downtown. I always remember the smell of*
> *cashews and chocolate.*

By the time he entered kindergarten, Chuck could read. Mrs. King was aware of her son's precociousness, and she provided him with books and comics to spur his interest. Your father's love of reading stuck with him all his life.

> *I love to read murder mysteries and stories about the 50s and early 60s. The most stunning book I've read is* Manchild in the Promised Land, *by Claude Browne. That book inspired me a lot and taught me no matter where you grow up, if you have determination and desire you can make it.*
>
> *I read the Bible when I was young but didn't really understand it until I became a man.*

Charles's mother encouraged his passion for art as well. He was in the first grade when he drew his first prize-winning picture, a portrait of a boy on a street corner holding a handful of balloons attached to invisible strings. "You have to use your imagination," he explained to his mother about the missing strings. The judges admired his ingenuity.

> *Grandma King entered me in the local art contest. I worked on my drawing while she continued to shop. I remember that I was so consumed with my drawing that I didn't want to leave. I got a phone call later that evening saying I won first place, a ribbon and ten dollars. Grandma King knew from then on what I had a passion for. Mom encouraged me every opportunity she could. Till this day I still enjoy doing*

*art for relaxation. It has been very rewarding for me
while I've been in the army. Thanks, God.*

As much as he adored his mother, Chuck revered his father.

*From my father I learned to be strong physically and
aggressive with every task given. Being in the army
you have to be a fire-breathing dragon sometimes.
I have to thank Dad for that quality. I'm sure you will
have great qualities also.*

Mr. King was a tall, lean, handsome man with dark eyes and
ebony skin. He cut an imposing figure, and his pressed slacks and
tailored suits offered no hint of his harsh beginnings in Sweet
Water, Alabama. Charles admired his father's work ethic and
resilience, and he loved to hear him laugh. He treasured the memory of skeet shooting with his father on a cousin's land in rural
Ohio.

*Dad was the image of a man to me. He was very
muscular, in great shape. I always felt that was the
way I should look and carry myself. Your grandpa was
very physical and loved to work outdoors in the yard,
around the house. All of the men on Grandpa's side of
the family were tall and physically tough.*

> *My father was a hard-working person who demanded to be treated as the equal of everyone else. I noticed that his friends were people who had backbone. Dad was really into the civil rights movement and made it clear that you should always be aware of what's going on in the political world.*

The Kings talked at the dinner table about the struggle for equality, although the emphasis was almost always on the positive. There was no discussion of the violence in Cleveland, which, like so many other American cities in that era, was rocked by racial ugliness and unrest. In July 1966, the tensions erupted. It happened in Hough, a disenfranchised neighborhood near downtown, a place of few jobs, rising crime, and shoddy housing that many residents and businesses had already abandoned. A black man went into a white bar and asked for water. The bartender refused, then posted a sign on the door: "No Water for Niggers." What began with words and shoves exploded into gunfire, arson, and looting, which became so relentless officials called in the National Guard to restore order. Firefighters battled hundreds of blazes, and hundreds of people were arrested. Millions of dollars in homes and businesses were destroyed. It took six terrifying nights for calm to return, and by then four people (including a young mother looking out the window of an apartment) were dead.

Charles knew little of the fury and pandemonium nearby. His parents had told him nothing of it. His school was on the eastern edge of the city and remained open, and although the couple drove through Hough to see the devastation, they decided to shield their children from it. Mrs. King told me she never wanted Charles and

Gail to have "bitterness about white people." When, years later, the family traveled to the South and stopped at a Holiday Inn or a Howard Johnson's, the Kings reminded their children that they hadn't always been allowed to patronize such places. But they never dwelled on it.

"Our parents never taught us that white people were racist or that there were obstacles," Gail recalled. "They just showed us to believe in ourselves. It was more about who *we* were. There was just no distinction between us and the white kids."

Yet they were not unrealistic, and the Kings did tell their son and daughter that the civil rights movement was fundamental to racial progress. They spoke with great pride of Rev. Martin Luther King Jr. (no relation to your father's family) and of Carl Stokes, who became the first black mayor of a major city when he was elected in Cleveland in 1967. They wanted their son and daughter to understand that there were good and bad people of all races. Their message was one of love, respect, and unity.

His parents' worldview shaped Charles's perspective in situations that might have left him bitter and defeated.

Son, every situation dealing with discrimination is somewhat different. Discrimination comes from people being ignorant or not knowing about a person's race or background.

I guess it's human nature for different cultures to profile one another. It's not fair to judge someone by the color of their skin, where they're raised, or their religious beliefs. Unless a person is rude or obnoxious,

*keep your opinions to yourself. You never know what
hidden talents a person might have to share with you.
  Life would be boring if we were all the same.
Appreciate people for who they are and learn from
their differences.*

Your grandmother still speaks vividly about the time that she shook hands with King during one of the leader's last trips to Cleveland. She can remember every moment: the frigid wind whipping off Lake Erie, the speech in which the civil rights leader rallied the crowd over the hiring practices at Sealtest, demanding the dairy company hire black milkmen and front office personnel. She remembers standing in line on that cold day, and finally grasping his hand.

"I thanked him for all the things he was doing to make our lives better," she told me. "He was so gracious; you'd think I was the person who was the big shot. I told Chuckie, 'The lesson here is that one person can make a difference.' That's what we tried to instill in him."

She also remembers your father's reaction when an assassin's bullet killed King a few months later: "Oh, he cried. We all cried. I told him that I felt like God called Martin Luther King home because he had done what he was supposed to do."

That day your grandparents knelt in prayer, something your father had seen them do often during his childhood. Your grandfather King, a deacon in their church, told his son many times how the power of prayer sustained him as a child growing up poor in the segregated South, with parents who had had no education.

> *Dad got on his knees every night and prayed to God. No man is too good to get on his knees and humble himself to God.*

Your father was proud of his dad's service in World War II, and proud that he'd completed a college degree at Tuskegee Institute. He remembered times when they had bonded without words, often just by watching TV together.

> *We had a black-and-white TV. I really liked* Voyage to the Bottom of the Sea *and* Star Trek. *Grandpa liked* Gunsmoke. *Every Sunday me and Grandpa would watch Abbott and Costello and Dean Martin and Jerry Lewis. I guess that was our comic relief.*

Your father does not spell out why he might have wished for relief, but I know there were some hard times. Early in our relationship, he confided that, when he was six or seven, he was abused by a relative who babysat for him. She yelled at him, pounded him in the head, and force-fed him frozen food. She often had sex with her boyfriend in front of him. Charles said he sought help from his parents but was unable to get them to listen. His parents say he never spoke about it, but Charles always insisted to me that he had tried to tell them. Throughout his life Charles hated red nail polish because he remembered seeing it on his babysitter's fingers as she undressed. I never wore it in his presence.

After your grandfather took in his ailing, diabetic mother,

Daisy King, and began working longer hours to pay for her care, Charles came to see his father as austere and aloof. The pressure of meeting her needs seemed to leave Mr. King little time or energy for his son.

> *Our family finances changed when my grandmother*
> *came to live with us. She had no medical insurance so*
> *Mom and Dad had to pay those bills.*
> *Dad always made sure we had something to eat.*
> *It wasn't until several years after my Grandma King*
> *passed that things started getting better financially*
> *for Mom and Dad. I knew my parents were struggling*
> *to make ends meet but they fought through it.*

The elder Mrs. King, a dark-skinned woman who had lived a hard life of servitude, was bitter and tired in her waning years. She did not hide her disdain for her daughter-in-law because of the younger woman's fair complexion. Such friction was common at the time, especially among blacks from the segregated South. Darker-toned blacks often resented the greater social access and more abundant job opportunities afforded to lighter-skinned blacks. They also resented the fact that some fair-skinned folks considered themselves a class above other blacks—especially those who could not pass the "paper bag test." People whose skin tones were darker than the color of the bag were often regarded as inferior—"field Negroes."

The tension permeated the household. There were times when Gladys drove the elder Mrs. King to medical appointments and the old lady refused to sit in the front seat beside her. Yet, to hear

Charles tell it, Gladys endured most of her mother-in-law's slights patiently. And she accepted the financial sacrifices they were forced to make. The Kings had at one time planned to move to a bigger house in a better neighborhood, but the medical bills meant that any money they had went toward the elder Mrs. King's care and toward their children's schooling.

The incident with his babysitter was not the only time your father felt alone with his pain. For a time his maternal grandmother also came to stay with the family—and one of the most traumatic events of your father's childhood was her death in the King home.

> *My most horrific experience was the day Grandma Freeman passed away in my room. She died in the morning before I went to school. When I got home my relatives were waiting so we could go to the funeral home to visit her for the last time. We arrived at the funeral home and went down to the basement. She was lying on the table covered up to her neck in a white sheet. She had beautiful white hair that was combed straight out. I was shocked to see her like that.*
>
> *My mother had sent Gail down the street to stay with neighbors while they went down south to bury my grandmother. I stayed at home with Grandma King. I was terrified to even go in my room. For more than a week I was afraid to even walk by my room, let alone go in it. Finally, a week later I couldn't take it anymore and went in my room and stayed until my fear subsided. I realized my grandmother would never do anything to hurt or frighten me. She loved me so much.*

Charles kept his pain to himself, which his mother attributed to selflessness. "He never gave us any trouble," she told me. "He kept things from me because he knew I worried so."

There was a price for that silence, however. Charles told me that he often felt as though he had no voice, and when he couldn't be heard, he just stopped talking. It became a lifelong defense mechanism.

So your father looked elsewhere for a place to be heard, and for someone to fill in as his dad became increasingly unavailable.

> *My hideaway was my best friend's home, Eddie Mason. That was like my second home.*

At the age of eleven or twelve, your father and Eddie were paperboys and shared a route. They shared little else, Charles being the obedient child who kept God first in his life and Eddie the neighborhood troublemaker, with no respect for authority. No one expected the friendship to last, but it did.

Even Eddie's own mother did not understand their bond.

"They were so different," Mattie Mason said. "I don't know what brought them together but my son really cared for him and he cared for my son. He was forever trying to keep Eddie out of trouble. He always tried to protect him and lead him down the right path. I remember him sitting on the steps and talking for hours with Eddie, trying to give him good advice. Eddie stayed out of trouble for most of his high school years thanks to Charles."

At the Masons, Charles also found another male role model, almost a surrogate father.

When Eddie left home, Mr. Mason kinda adopted me. I could talk to Mr. Mason about things I was afraid to talk to Grandpa King about. Until the day I left home to go to college, Mr. Mason was always there for me. When I needed money for a school dance or a car for the prom, Mr. Mason would let me work for him. He even took me to the mall to get my suit for the school dance. Mr. Mason was a good man. He always steered me in the right direction.

Mr. Mason was the one with answers to questions about matters that were simply not discussed in the King household.

Son, if you want to know anything about sex, please ask me. Grandpa King didn't talk about it, so I had to go to the library or ask Mr. Mason. Don't be afraid to ask me.

After Charles left Cleveland for college, Eddie Mason, who had by then taken up with a group of thugs and was no longer living with his parents, was adrift without his only true friend. Eddie was killed in a drug-related shooting at the age of twenty-two. Charles's grief was palpable. He was angry, too. The first time he visited his friend's gravesite, he told him off, saying that he had wasted his life and hurt the people he had loved.

"He acted like he lost a brother," Mrs. Mason said. Anytime he came home to Cleveland, Charles would come by to check on the

Masons, and on Valentine's Day, Mother's Day, and Christmas, he would send cards he had made himself. For years he would say apologetically, "I tried, I tried."

Other than the Masons, one of the places where your father felt most relaxed and protected as a child was the Lee Heights Community Church, a sanctuary of about three hundred members. It was a single-story brick building, modest except for its towering stained-glass windows behind the pulpit. The Kings had searched for nearly two years for the right church before settling on Lee Heights. They chose it because they believed in the Reverend Vern Miller, a diminutive white man with giant convictions, and because it was one of the very few churches where black and white worshipped together. Miller preached racial unity and involvement in the community, two of the Kings' most deeply held ideals.

Mrs. King noticed the allure of crime and drugs for some of the neighborhood kids with too much idle time, and got Charles involved in the church as a way to keep him from falling prey to the same influences. She sent him to summer camp with other children from the congregation, urged him to attend Bible study, and encouraged him to join the youth choir. She also hoped that attending Sunday school and being part of the choir would help with her son's reticence.

I joined my church around the age of twelve. That was a big deal for my family. It was a Methodist church, and it was unusual for my neighborhood because it was integrated. My earliest memories were of being in the church choir. I didn't want to do it, but my parents

> *encouraged it. I wasn't really good at singing and*
> *I was a bit bashful about being in front of people.*
> *It made life interesting though. It helped me to interact*
> *with members of the church who were my age.*

"Even as a teen, he didn't mind waking up early Sunday morning to go to church. He had it in him. He had the spirit," Gail recalled.

I envied Charles his Christian upbringing and believed his faith had everything to do with his buoyancy and his composure. I cherished the image of him in a crisp white shirt and tie on his way to church, and of him hiding behind his hymnal every time he had to sing before the congregation. We read the Bible when I was a child and prayed over meals and at bedtime, but my father did not trust organized religion and said he was doing us a favor by not bringing us up in a church. I never believed him, and I wondered how different I might have been with a solid spiritual foundation, or with a mentor like Charles's Pastor Miller.

> *Rev. Vern Miller was a very quiet and humble man, but*
> *he had courage you could not imagine. He was the only*
> *white pastor in my neighborhood. His home was always*
> *open to us. When we had family problems he invited me*
> *and your Aunt Gail to spend the evening at his home.*

Recently, Miller spoke of the kinship he felt with Charles. "He reminded me of my own childhood," he said. "I was a shy kid.

He spoke only when you spoke to him, but when he did reply he was very courteous and respectful."

Charles and Miller shared a reverence for the Bible, and your father developed a deep understanding of the scriptures that would sustain him all his life. "Every Sunday he read the Bible," Miller said. "He was very diligent. Both his parents took God seriously and he tended to be very eager to follow that example. That was his character."

During the time Charles and I were together, he often would cite Bible verses when we were confronted with difficult decisions. He was the only man I ever prayed with.

I always prayed as a boy and still pray every day. The one specific prayer I remember was asking God to give me a sister. Then Grandma King had your Aunt Gail. My parents taught me to pray. I watched them get on their knees and pray before they went to bed. I used to say the Lord's Prayer every night. Now I pray every morning. Prayer works.

Your father said often that he believed his artistic talent as well as his outstanding athletic abilities were divine gifts. He received a gold medal in track and lettered in football and wrestling—which evidently came as a surprise to your grandfather.

He started to attend some of my football games and track meets. I don't think he realized how hard

> *I worked to be a good athlete. I will never forget*
> *after one track meet he shook my hand and said,*
> *"Son, I didn't know you could do all those things."*
> *It was sad.*

Your father's athleticism did not escape the notice of the girls at school.

"He was one good-looking boy," recalled Kimberly Mack, a high school girlfriend who is now a middle school teacher in Cleveland. "A lot of girls liked him."

Charles's friendship with Kimberly turned romantic during their sophomore year. "I used to wonder if he would ever kiss me," she said. "It took him a good while. He was probably the most respectful guy I have ever dated—ever. He never pushed me more than I was willing to go. He always made sure I got home at the time my parents wanted me home."

The courtship lasted just a few months, but the friendship endured—even after Charles began dating one of her friends.

"It kind of happened and then it just melted away," Kimberly said. "He was not a player. We were probably the only two girlfriends he had in school." Kimberly still has a picture of her and Charles with their classmates. He is standing in the back, on the outskirts. "He always kept to himself," she said. "While all the other guys were out ripping and running, he was a lot quieter."

On occasion, though, she saw flashes of temper. "I remember one time someone was teasing one of the kids. He got all in his face. Here was this nice guy and all of a sudden he was roaring. He never, ever raised his voice, so to see that was a shock."

As a young man who respected authority and craved structure, your father had always been enthralled with the military. In fact, if he had had his way, he would have embarked on a military career much sooner than he did.

> *I tried to get Grandma King to send me to a military academy. She wasn't hearing it. I wanted to start my military career while I was in junior high. I was looking forward to the discipline and esprit de corps that the military academy would offer. I thought it would be challenging and fun. Plus I could get away from home.*

In their work at the VA hospital, the Kings had seen too many maimed and scarred veterans to be comfortable with the prospect of their son ending up among them—or worse. After Charles graduated from high school in 1977, Mrs. King persuaded him not to join the military. Ever the obedient son, he pursued a career as a commercial artist, earning an associate's degree in art from a junior college in Boston and studying at the Art Institute of Chicago. He attended the school from 1979 to 1983, when he ran out of money just a few classes short of graduating.

Charles went to work as an illustrator for a Chicago publishing company, creating art for phone book advertisements, but found the work unsatisfying. In late 1983, he headed south to Mobile, Alabama, where he had relatives, and got a job as a commercial artist at a local newspaper. But office life never suited your father. Unlike the military, there was no rulebook, and he was bewildered by the ruthless politics. He was passed over for a promotion after someone questioned whether he had actually earned his associate's degree. Deeply hurt, he quit after just six months and spent the next few years working at a string of unrewarding jobs.

In 1985, Charles met Cecilia—also an artist—and promptly fell in love. He hoped to marry her, provided he could figure out a way to support them both. Once again he found himself drawn to the military, and this time he did not consult his parents first. But he did tell them after he had visited a recruiter, and his mother was able to talk him out of training to be a paratrooper on the grounds that it was "too dangerous and strenuous." His second choice was the air force but, at twenty-nine, he was a year too old to enlist. So your father took an entrance exam and a physical and joined the army.

On October 13, 1987, Charles swore an oath to protect and defend his country and became Private First Class King. "They cleared him to go, and the next thing I knew he was gone," his mother said. He married Cecilia two months later.

Military service fulfilled Charles in a way that nothing else did. He was a tank crew commander early in his career and then a drill sergeant for four years. He was steadily promoted: staff sergeant, platoon sergeant, master sergeant. As a tank gunner during Operation Desert Storm, he destroyed three Iraqi armored vehicles, earning a Bronze Star. In 1992 he was sent to Kuwait on a security mission. Three years later he worked as the senior noncommissioned officer in Guantanamo Bay, leading a humanitarian mission to aid Cuban refugees who had fled their island nation by sea. He was ultimately promoted to first sergeant—the second highest rank an enlisted soldier can attain, putting him on track for a final promotion to sergeant major. Along the way, Charles earned a chestful of medals for his valor.

It seemed natural that your father's love of the military would find expression in his art. Although his subjects varied widely, he was proudest of his work depicting African Americans' contributions to the military. He became fascinated by the history of the 761st Tank Battalion, an unsung unit of black soldiers that fought fiercely in World War II, and created a series of pointillist collages depicting members of the unit as young soldiers and as old men. He said he chose that style because the veterans deserved the time and attention to detail it took to draw each illustration. He loaned ten such drawings to the Pentagon in 1998, where they were displayed during Black History Month, and his work is on permanent display at the Fort Lewis Military Museum near Tacoma, Washington, and at several other bases across the country. More important, he got to present the surviving 761st tankers with autographed copies of the portraits.

> *One of the nicest things I ever did was invite my parents to a conference room dedicated to the 761st Tank Battalion in Fort Knox, Kentucky. They had a great time and got to meet some of the actual members of the 761st. They were very proud. Both your mother's parents and my parents were present to witness the conference room dedication. That same exhibit is hanging up in five locations in the country. Fort Hood, Texas, will be its next home.*

The man who longed to be needed had found his calling as a military leader.

Even so, there were notes of dissent. However proud, his family never entirely understood his choice, and his former pastor was even more puzzled.

"I was mystified by his military career," Rev. Vern Miller said.

"His parents explained to me that they both worked for the government and the government was good to them. I was told Chuck was denied a promotion in the private sector where he worked and was looking for an alternative. Because he tended to trust the government, he chose the military."

Charles understood the doubts, and had an answer for them. When the church youth director asked why a kid from a church that encourages peace would go the military route, Charles considered the question for a moment. Then he said:

"Because the military needs Christians, too."

Four

Dear Jordan,

Charles's and my courtship began with a phone call. From my father.

Although my dad had given up liquor years earlier, his voice on my answering machine sounded strangely giddy. "Hey, Punkin," he said, calling me by the childhood nickname I have always loathed. "Just wanted to let you know that Charles asked me for your phone number. I gave it to him. Hope you don't mind."

I cringed. My father was playing matchmaker.

The truth is, I had thought about Charles for a few days after I returned to New York from Kentucky, but not much in the three weeks since. Our encounter had been pleasant but fleeting. He was sweet, handsome, and obviously principled, but I wasn't in a dating mood.

That spring I had broken up with my boyfriend of two and a half years, and I had not gone out with a man since. Greg was the managing editor of the *Boston Globe* and twelve years my senior. He was a tall, chocolate-colored charmer with the face and voice of a television news anchor—the only person I knew who loved newspapers more than I did. We discussed books and social issues and, of course, news. He introduced me to cigars and single malt scotch and gave me a copy of Katherine Graham's autobiography. He took me on vacations to Martha's Vineyard, where we ate lobster and played Scrabble on a private beach.

Our relationship was intense—and combustible. I was insecure about holding my own with a man of his stature and felt more like his pupil than his partner. Greg was preoccupied with our age difference and frustrated that our careers kept us in different cities. In time he became distant. When he bought a house without consulting me less than a year after I moved to New York, I knew we would never live in it together. I left him before he had a chance to leave me.

Even so, I took the breakup hard. (It was the only time I ever lost my appetite over a man.) I was not looking to replace Greg when Charles came along, and certainly not with someone so unlike him.

Yet a few days after my father's message, there was another one.

"Hi Dana, this is Sergeant King," Charles said. "I got your number from your dad. Give me a call when you have time."

He sounded stiff and formal. I called him back the following day, just to be polite.

"Sergeant King," he answered, and I was instantly conscious of how little interest I had in dating a soldier.

"Hi, this is Dana."

"Hey, how are you?"

"Fine. And you?"

We were as warm as two people on a telemarketing cold call.

The conversation turned to the weather in New York, then to how hard we had both been working. I tried to wrap things up by saying it was nice of him to phone.

"I've thought about giving you a call ever since you left Kentucky," he persisted. "I've just been busy at work and dealing with my personal situation."

I knew he was referring to his divorce and wanted to ask why he was interested in me at such a tumultuous time in his life, but I did not want to make him feel like the subject of a news story. I was also not so sure about my own motives. Maybe I was simply looking for a candy man—a sweet treat to ease my loneliness.

Despite my misgivings, Charles and I kept talking after that initial call. At first I told him more about the New York subway system than about myself. He talked about military history, but stayed away from the subject of his broken marriage. They were easy, first-date discussions, but without the dates. He said he admired the French artist Erté. I said I loved anything by Langston Hughes. We discovered that our birthdays were two days apart and that we both liked chocolate—one of us in moderation, the other in abundance.

As that smoldering July became an even hotter August, we began speaking every night. Our conversations turned introspective. We talked about his daughter and about my choice to have a career before a family. In time, I began to look forward to his calm, steady voice being the last thing I heard before I slept.

We became friends.

Charles revealed, with some prodding, that he considered the collapse of his marriage to be the biggest failure of his life. Before he and Cecilia wed, he said, they had shared big dreams—dreams of pursuing their art and eventually starting a family. They had dreamed of saving enough money to make a down payment on a house, maybe even enough to travel or buy a new car. Afterward, he came to feel that they did not share the same goals and values. Through much of their marriage he was the sole breadwinner, and there were times when he wished she contributed more financially.

They never did manage to buy a home, and by the end of the marriage, too much trust had been broken.

I only knew his side of the story, but I could tell how wounded and ashamed he felt. He said he had prayed hard that the marriage could be salvaged before he finally decided it was over. He was most concerned about the consequences for his daughter. I urged him to give her time to adjust to such a difficult change in her life. I reminded him that he had suffered a huge loss, too, and should give himself permission to grieve. Mostly, I listened.

> *Your mother spent so much time pulling me out of being depressed from a failed marriage that I couldn't help but fall in love with her. She helped me overcome a lot of personal obstacles.*

As Charles opened up, I did, too. I told him about the pressure of being a black woman in a high-profile position at the *New York Times*. It was not just that I felt there would be no second chances if I messed up, it was that I sometimes felt like a standard bearer for all African American journalists who aspired to work at the *Times*. I also never got used to the awkward moments when a white banker or politician I had cultivated as a source on the phone met me and seemed shocked that I was black.

I told Charles about sometimes feeling alone in a city of seven million people. I told him how tough it was to grow up as the eldest daughter of an autocratic drill sergeant and a mother who was too fragile to stand up to him. I also confided something I had told very few people: For as long as I could remember, my dad had told his children the sort of obscene jokes that should have been reserved for his soldiers. I would lower my head in embarrassment and say they were not funny, which would make him laugh harder.

"I was a drill sergeant, too, and I would never talk to my daughter like that," Charles said one evening. "No father should."

With those words, I felt a brick loosen in the wall around me. Finally, here was a man who validated my feelings about one of the most uncomfortable and confusing experiences of my life. He was angry for me, which made me begin to think that, just maybe, I could trust him.

I told Charles that the entire town of Radcliff had known of my father's mistress and that he had made little attempt to hide his affair. In fact, I was the only one of the children who refused to meet her. Most evenings, after dinner, my father would announce that he was going for milk while my mother sat solemnly, head lowered, never questioning him about where he was really headed. It was generally well after midnight when his car pulled back into the driveway; the sound of the engine often woke me. My dad even said that he had never loved my mother and had only married her because she was pregnant and so poor and mistreated that she slept on two chairs she had pushed together to make a bed. My dad said she had "trapped" him by having so many kids and had her own secrets besides. He never said what she was supposedly hiding but often alluded to her having other men and remarked that at least he owned up to his mistakes.

No matter how bad the marriage, I knew my mother would never leave. She had no money, was a high school dropout, and had five children. It seemed to me that she was the one who was trapped. I vowed never to allow myself to be in the same position.

"The way I grew up shaped my views about men," I explained to Charles. "I've had my guard up for so long that I don't know what it feels like to lower it."

Charles seemed to understand. He was careful not to move too fast, and I was enjoying the crush I had developed on him from a safe distance. Then, during one of our nightly talks, he said he wanted to know more about New York City. Flirtatiously, I said, "Let me show you *my* city."

"Okay, when can I come visit?" he asked, seizing his opening.

"Um, I don't know" was all I could manage.

"I have a four-day pass in two weeks. Want me to see if I can find a ticket?"

"Sure, I guess so."

It was becoming clear to me that, in his own unassuming way, Charles pursued what he wanted, which apparently was me. He said he had always admired strong women and liked my independence and the sense of purpose I drew from my career. He also thought I was beautiful—hips and all.

> *I expect a woman to be honorable, to take care of herself and take pride in how she looks and carries herself. But beauty is in the eye of the beholder. I expect a woman to be a great communicator who will guard and cherish your friendship first. I expect a woman to be intellectually stimulating no matter what her background may be. Look at your mother; that will tell you what I like in a woman.*

Despite myself, I had become smitten, too. He was a homebody and a family man. The weekend we met, he had been sweet with my six-year-old niece: when she giggled and asked to see his muscles, Charles lifted the squealing girl off the ground on his arm instead of flexing his biceps. And he had sat beside my father on the front porch, patiently listening to his old army stories. This was a man who adored children and respected his elders.

If only he were a civilian. If only he were a news junkie. If only he did not live so far away.

My father did not say it at the time, but he had hoped from the start that my budding friendship with Charles would develop into something more. He believed Charles was worthy of his feisty daughter's affections.

"He had an inner strength that I knew was stone-cold soldier and stone-cold man," my dad said later. "And he had compassion and a soft side."

Even though I had grown up as the daughter of a military man, I did not yet understand the strength of character it took to be a career soldier, and I had no interest in that side of Charles. As the time of his visit drew near, all I could think was: *He won't be in uniform, but he's still a soldier. Why am I doing this?*

Two nights before Charles's visit, I went out for drinks with my friend Mia and we discussed my potential new man. Mia, a reporter on the Metro desk, was like a big sister. I needed her advice.

"So do you like this guy?" she asked, sipping her Cosmo.

"I guess I do," I said. "But he's not exactly my type. I mean, what if I have to introduce him to the executive editor at a *Times* event? He mispronounces words and doesn't keep up with the news."

Mia rolled her lovely brown eyes and set down her glass.

"Listen," she said, "how many *Times* parties do you go to with the executive editor anyway? And who cares if Charles doesn't speak perfect English? You said he was nice, right?"

I looked away, ashamed for putting on such airs. I was a girl from Kentucky who had not even owned a suit when I went on my first job interview. For years I memorized new words in the dictionary to expand my vocabulary, and I never was any good with fractions. I worked two jobs in college to afford books and food and never came close to making the Dean's List. Who did I think I was? A big shot who was too good for this big-hearted man?

There was something else, though. I still loved Greg.

Mia reminded me that he was seeing someone else. "It's time for you to move on, too," she said. "Just see what happens with Charles."

She was right. I should at least give Charles a chance.

On the phone, the night before he arrived, I gingerly brought up the issue of sleeping arrangements. I told him I had a sofa bed, and he said that, of course, that was where he would sleep. I was relieved.

"What did you think I expected?" he said, laughingly.

"I don't know," I lied, "I just don't want to set up any unrealistic expectations."

It sounded silly even as I said it. The man was getting on a plane to spend the weekend in my home. I knew that this was the beginning of more than a friendship.

I quickly switched subjects, giving him directions to my apartment from LaGuardia Airport. I made him read them back to me and then told him how much the cab ride should cost and how much to tip the driver.

"But only if he helps you with your bags," I instructed.

"Yes, ma'am," Charles said, seeming amused.

This man had fought in Desert Storm and I was worried about him taking a taxi into Manhattan! We hung up and I lay in bed staring at the ceiling a long time, thinking about how different Charles and I were and how it did not seem to bother him the way it did me. If anything, he was intrigued by our differences.

*I know your mother hates for me to say she is strong,
but she really is strong. Most people wait for the storm
to come to them. Your mother stepped through it and
challenged every obstacle. She certainly has achieved
her goals with a great deal of modesty. I always
admired her for living in New York City, especially
with the competitive profession she decided to pursue.*

I was not a soldier the way your father was, but there were moments when I felt as if I were on the front lines, too. As a *New York Times* business reporter who covered the finances, management, and product development of some of the largest corporations in the world—Procter & Gamble, McDonald's, and Gillette among them—I had dined with the chief executives of Fortune 500 companies. I had written articles that moved their companies' stocks on Wall Street.

It was intense, rewarding work, but it was not the career I would have predicted for myself. As a young girl, I had written poems and short stories. I would lose myself in them for hours, forgetting the pain and confusion of arguments between my parents that ended with my mother trembling and in tears and my father heading out the door. In my high school scrapbook, I wrote that a decade after graduation I would be a writer in New York City, but I wasn't thinking of reporting. I envisioned myself writing novels that would plumb hard truths about class and race and offer piercing insights into the dynamics between men and women—or fathers and daughters.

Being practical, though, I majored in journalism at the University of Kentucky, which put me on a path to a writing career with job security and health benefits. During the summers, I worked at newspapers, including the *Plain Dealer* in Cleveland in 1986 and the *Wall Street Journal* the following summer. Then I got a job after college as a police reporter at the *Palm Beach Post* in Florida.

That hot, miserable year made me much tougher: I drove into an approaching hurricane to write about an evacuation and went on drug raids with the police. But I was lonesome and missed the change of seasons. And I never got used to those god-awful little lizards everywhere.

Still, I liked nothing better than covering a juicy murder trial, so when the *Plain Dealer* approached me about a similar job in 1989, I headed to the Midwest. I thrived. Cops would try to shake up the crime reporters, but they quickly saw that they couldn't faze me. I once spent a day in prison interviewing a murderer, who casually explained how to produce "instant death, very little blood" by sticking a knife into a particular spot at the base of the skull. But I was best with grieving families. I cared, and they could tell.

I stayed at the *Plain Dealer* for eight years, until the mid 1990s, when I met some reporters and editors from the *Times* at a journalism convention and they invited me to New York for a round of interviews. The *Times* eventually made an offer, but three things weighed on my mind.

The first was that New York was expensive and loud and overwhelming. In Cleveland I had a fabulous apartment overlooking Lake Erie and a convertible sports car that helped me get dates. I had an active social life and, for the first time, a savings account.

Then there was the fact that the *Times* offer came with a huge caveat. It was an apprentice reporting position in which I would have three years to prove I was "*Times*worthy" or be let go.

Finally, there was Greg, who wanted me to move to Boston,

not to New York. I wanted to be with him, too, but I had fears of being stuck in Boston with no job and only a man's money to rely on. I had a recurring nightmare in which my real life turned out to have been a dream and I woke up with no education and no job.

But what if I accepted the job at the *Times,* lost Greg, and failed the apprenticeship?

I was torn. So I consulted the only friend I trusted to advise me about the decision—Greg's mother.

Geneva Moore was approaching seventy but still dyed her hair red and went dancing in black leather pants. She was a dame, and I adored her. We spent hours on the phone talking about her life as a young woman and my career. When I told her that I was close to taking a job at the *Times* and that the decision would likely lead to the end of my relationship with her son, I knew she would not hold back.

"The *New York Times?*" Geneva Moore said excitedly. "Dana, I love you and I love my son, but he could get hit by a bus. Honey, you better take that job."

I accepted the position that week in the summer of 1996, along with the uncertainty that came with it.

There was an intoxicating energy to New York City, just as there was in the newsroom, and I adapted to it quickly. I made friends with some of the younger reporters, and we plotted our careers after hours at restaurants and bars near our Midtown office that served designer cocktails and tiny appetizers on giant plates.

Professionally, the risk paid off: just a year later, in the fall of 1997, I was promoted out of the apprentice program.

Now here I was on a Friday morning, this tough career woman, putting on a gray skirt suit instead of the jeans and blazer I usually wore at the end of the week. I put a makeup kit and perfume in my briefcase. I slipped my feet into a pair of painful black pumps, deciding to suffer through the agony instead of wearing comfortable loafers. I had bought fresh flowers on the way home the day before and set them out in vases around my apartment. All for a man I was still not sure I wanted.

Late in the afternoon I was in the newsroom writing a story on deadline and had almost forgotten about his flight. Then Charles called. He had made it to my building and gotten the key I left with the doorman. I told him I would be a few hours.

"No problem. I brought my sketch pad," he said.

By the time I had finished my piece and made it home on the subway, it was nearly eight. Charles was sitting in my living room, drawing. When he stood up, I felt the same flutter in my stomach I had when we first met. He was scrumptious.

He smiled shyly and we hugged. I lingered in his arms and looked into his face. We kissed lightly, a tentative peck that felt like a beginning. It was enough to make me forget about deadlines and traffic. I was home.

Shy is not a word that describes me, but I was oddly nervous. I had pretended to be the sort of woman who would casually invite a man to her home for a weekend, but I did not feel casual about things at all. Charles was there because I wanted him to be.

"Let me show you my city," I said, trying to relax. "Isn't that why you're here?"

Charles chuckled and I met his gaze with a playful smile that seemed to put us both at ease. We took the subway to a romantic Italian restaurant, not overly fancy, where we sat by an open window.

I had learned more about Charles in the past month than I had about some men I had dated for the better part of a year, but it had been a phone relationship. Sitting face-to-face with an entire weekend stretched out before us was disconcerting. I was relieved when the waiter broke the silence by offering us bread and pouring oil into a dish.

"What's that, butter?" Charles asked.

"No, olive oil," I said. He seemed embarrassed.

Charles watched me dip a chunk of the warm crusty bread into the dish and take a bite. When he declined a slice, I was not sure whether the olive oil was too great a novelty for him or whether he was simply steering clear of carbohydrates. I ordered linguini with clam sauce—more carbs. Charles ordered a salad.

"Give us a minute," I instructed the waiter.

"Charles, you can eat salad anywhere," I said. "Why don't you try the pasta? They make it from scratch here." On the army base, I knew, he generally ate cafeteria food, and I suspected that if he had pasta at home, it was ravioli from a can. This was a chance to relax and be adventuresome, if only for a weekend. I wanted him to enjoy himself.

"But I want a salad," Charles insisted.

"Well at least have some grilled chicken on it or something."

He shrugged his shoulders and agreed to add a skinless chicken breast. I didn't know then how strictly he watched his diet; I saw it as a sign that he was rigid or afraid to try new things.

"So have you seen my parents lately?" I asked, wishing we could both loosen up. He said that he had, and we laughed about how shocked they would be to know that he was visiting me. We had decided not to tell our families about our courtship until we knew ourselves whether there was anything worth telling.

I wanted so badly for Charles to be comfortable that I reached across the table and rubbed his arm. "I really am glad you're here," I said softly. "We're going to have a great time getting to know each other better."

Charles leaned over the table and kissed me on the lips. I tasted a hint of oregano, one of my favorite spices, and leaned in for more. Finally, we were relaxed enough to enjoy our first official date. The glow lasted until the check arrived.

I knew that I made more money than him and that he had a daughter to support. I suspected that he could not afford the hundred-dollar meal. So I told him that since he had just bought a round-trip ticket to New York, this was my treat. Still, he seemed uncomfortable when I discreetly slid the bill in my direction. He wiped his mouth with the cloth napkin and said nothing as I handed the waiter a credit card.

It occurred to me that perhaps he was the sort of man who still believed in the dating rituals of a bygone era. I was right. The entire weekend, Charles insisted on being on the curb side of the sidewalk to put distance between me and the traffic. It was a sweet, throwback gesture that in any other city I would have appreciated, but it drove me crazy as we tried to keep pace with the rushed pedestrians on New York's one-way streets and congested avenues. He had to step in front of or behind me every few blocks to switch positions in order to come between me and the traffic.

"Charles, please stop that," I said as patiently as I could when we approached yet another packed intersection. "I appreciate you looking out for me, but you can't do that in New York. You'd have to switch sides practically every block."

He smiled and shook his head in agreement but he never did stop dodging dogs and drivers and pedestrians to make that loving gesture. I eventually stopped fighting it, realizing how important it was to him and how blessed I was that a man cared enough about me to make it. The last time I ever walked with him, pushing a stroller on our way back from dinner at a Chinese restaurant, Charles gently tapped me on the hip every few blocks, a signal I knew well. I instinctively responded by stepping in front of him so he could switch positions: a dance born of his gentility that we had long ago perfected.

> Chivalry is not dead. A gentleman is someone who treats a woman with respect. It's the little things like opening doors, walking on the outside of the sidewalk to protect her from traffic and giving up your seat to an elderly person or pregnant woman. A gentleman exemplifies character; he treats his woman like she is the most beautiful creature on earth. A gentleman is always in defense mode for his woman. He will never let any harm come to her and he will never do anything to harm her. Try it; she will treat you like a king.

It took a while for me to learn to let Charles fuss over me, especially when we both knew I was capable of taking care of myself. In time I realized that accepting his overtures was not a threat to my independence but rather confirmation of how secure I was with it.

There was still a hint of daylight when we made our way out onto the street that evening, and I threw my hand up to hail a cab. As a taxi pulled over, Charles looked uncomfortable, and I realized that he had wanted to signal it himself. It was too late, so we slid into the backseat and I told the driver to take us to Times Square. I could not wait to show your father the sights—the gigantic neon billboards, the historic Broadway theaters, the *New York Times* building—but he seemed brooding and distracted. It probably didn't help that, without thinking, I paid the fare. At least I thought to wait for Charles to help me out of the cab.

We strolled, holding hands as I pointed out various landmarks. I am not a petite woman, but my hand felt tiny in his. His grip was strong and I could feel the tightness of his muscles squeezing my fingers.

Living in New York requires a certain edge, which I acquired by osmosis. Guards are rarely let down, motives almost always questioned. I had grown accustomed to being vigilant to protect myself without depending on a man. Now here was this massive man making me feel as safe as I did on the front porch of my parents' house in Kentucky.

Charles was polite enough as we walked, but by the end of the night he was very quiet. I hoped that in city-girl mode I did not seem too unlike the relaxed woman he had met in my parents' living room. Perhaps he was simply as nervous as I was about what would come next.

I offered him a beer when we returned home and excused myself to take a shower. He still had more than half a bottle when I rejoined him in the living room wearing a T-shirt and a pair of baggy shorts. My reporter friend Rachel had given me advice on how to handle this potentially awkward part of the evening.

"Just don't shave your legs. That way you won't get into trouble."

She was serious. I'm the girly-girl in my circle of friends and Rachel knew I would never sleep with a man, at least not the first time, without exfoliating, shaving, and moisturizing my skin.

I sat next to Charles on my black leather couch and tucked my legs under me to hide the stubble. He yawned a few times and took another few sips of beer. He probably would have sat there all night rather than suggest going to bed for fear that I would misinterpret his intentions.

I had had a long week and was tired, too. "If you don't mind, I'm ready to turn in. You can either sleep on the couch or on one side of my bed," I finally said, impulsively putting aside the sleeping arrangements we had agreed upon. It sounded like something a teenager would propose, but I was not sure what else to say. I wanted him near me, but not too close.

I stood up and Charles followed me into my bedroom. He grabbed his toiletries out of his suitcase and went to the bathroom. I slid into bed and pulled the covers up to my neck. What had I been thinking, inviting him into my bed on what was, in essence, our first date?

Charles came back in the bedroom with a sheepish smile on his face and got into bed wearing a tank top and gym shorts. He looked out of place, this brawny soldier lying there in my wrought-iron canopy bed outfitted with pink sheets and draped with delicate lavender sheers. We met in the middle and he took me in his arms. When his lips met mine I remembered why he was there, even as I wondered how I could ever be with a man who only ate salad.

We kissed long and hard before I gently pushed him away.

"We should stop," I said, breathing heavily.

He laid his head on my chest and then said he did not mean to get carried away. We slid to our respective sides of the bed, pretending to fall asleep. I remained awake for the longest time, and I suspected he did, too.

Lots of people start relationships in lust and end up in disaster. Passion is an attraction to someone for their qualities, how they think, how you interact with each other, how you spend quality time with each other and the ways you make each other happy. You enjoy being with that person not just for the physical side; that's

> *just the icing on the cake. It is a way of showing how*
> *you feel about your companion. Passion is great when*
> *you find that special person in your life. . . . Sex didn't*
> *mean anything to me until I was with my girlfriend in*
> *college. I really cared about that person, and that's*
> *what made it special. I recommend you wait until you*
> *are mature and understand what the consequences*
> *could be, whether emotional, pregnancy, or diseases.*

I awoke the next morning to a tapping sound on the floor and opened my eyes, squinting. I lifted my head. Charles was on the floor, doing push-ups on a set of metal handrails he had brought with him.

"I'm sorry, I tried to be quiet," he said.

"Oh my God, who gets up this early on a Saturday?" I said, trying to sit up. "And who travels with portable gym equipment?"

"It's not early," he said laughing. "It's almost nine o'clock."

I grunted and slid back down in bed. Charles walked out of the room and returned a minute later with two glasses of orange juice. I was awake enough to notice that his neck and chest were glistening with perspiration.

"My God, you have an amazing body," I said.

He smiled and leaned over to kiss me. "Thank you," he said.

He told me he was going running. I rolled back over, told him where I had put my keys, and said I was going back to sleep. When I woke up more than an hour later, he had returned and was stretching vigorously on the floor beside me. No Martian could have looked more alien to me.

"Seriously, don't you ever sleep in on weekends?"

"I get up at five during the week," he said.

A military man, indeed.

Staying in bed until noon would have been rude, so I pulled myself together enough to play tour guide for a second day. Charles was struck by the usual touristy things—the way the height of the buildings obscured the sun for entire blocks, the smell of honey-roasted cashews sold hot from a street cart, the subway musician blowing a trumpet so sweetly in a humid underground tunnel. I tried to point out things the tourists did not always see. He blinked in disbelief when I showed him a grocery store that only sold low-fat and fat-free foods. He all but giggled when he bit into a pastry from a popular bakery in my neighborhood. I kissed powdered sugar off his lips.

"That tasted good," he said. "I like the pastry, too."

I wrapped my arms around his neck and we kissed again as customers brushed past us with their coffee and muffins.

"What do you want to do next?" I asked him when we made our way back onto the street.

"Whatever you want," he said. "I'm all yours."

"Please," I said. "I'm trying to be a good girl."

He curled his lips into a mischievous smile.

"I know a lovely fountain, a wall of water cut right into the middle of a busy block. Want to see it?"

He nodded and took my hand.

"You know, I don't think I can show you everything in one weekend," I said, playfully glancing at him out of the corner of my eye.

In the months that followed, Charles visited two or three more times and gradually became a part of my life. Our feelings for each other went beyond friendship, and we had become more physical, but we still had not defined the relationship.

We shopped for clothes in New York to replace his oversize T-shirts and baggy jeans: pleated slacks and knit shirts, jeans that hugged him nicely, leather loafers and sandals to replace his sneakers. As long as he was out of uniform and away from the military base, it was almost possible for me to forget that he was a soldier.

I did not visit Fort Riley. It was not a place I was anxious to see, and my latest assignment left little time for leisure travel. If we remained in my world, he was simply Charles, the handsome man who had become my steady companion.

I took him to the Metropolitan Museum of Art, Broadway plays, and Central Park. We spread out on the city's great lawn one weekend with a picnic basket and I teasingly said, after he had unpacked our food and books, that the spot he had chosen was all wrong. He wanted so badly to please me that he twice packed up our belongings and relocated until I was satisfied.

"You know," he said, "you would be shocked to see me with my soldiers, and they would be shocked to see me with you."

I did not think his men had ever seen him catering to the whims of a woman, but it would be years before I would know just *how* different Charles the military leader was from Charles the man I would come to adore.

I flew up to see your mother. . . . This particular visit we decided to have a picnic in Central Park. Yes, son, we had a picnic basket with sandwiches and something to drink. The first place we chose was pretty lumpy, so we moved. The second spot was on an incline, so we moved. The third spot was just right and we enjoyed our outing in Central Park. Very romantic; we had a great evening.

By late fall I had introduced Charles to most of my friends. We hosted a small cocktail party on a Friday night when the chill in the air hinted at the changing season. Charles turned on some jazz and I hummed as I blanched carrots and sugar peas for crudités and asked him to put fruit and cheese on a platter.

"Dana, will you be my girlfriend?" he asked.

"Where did *that* come from?" I asked. I had not expected to have a "relationship" talk.

He looked wounded.

"Charles, you know I care about you," I said. "Why do we have to define our relationship?"

He simply looked down and sliced more cheese.

I felt guilty and confused. So many women, especially black women, longed for the affections of an honorable man—a man so sweet that he was actually asking me to go steady!

I had to be honest with myself about why I was holding back. My ideal man, I thought, looked like Charles but wore a suit to work and carried the *Wall Street Journal* under his arm. He was as comfortable discussing the stock market on a golf course as he was trash-talking on a basketball court. We were just so different, Charles and me. We had started out at roughly the same place in life, his beginnings slightly more middle class than mine. But now I lived in a different world.

It was not that Charles could not adapt to my world; I liked introducing him to it, but there were tensions. One evening several weeks earlier, I had gone down to meet him in the lobby of the *Times*. I got off the elevator and looked around. Then I saw him lurking behind a giant bust of our former publisher, practically hiding—something not lost on the security guards, who were keeping close watch over him. Why was he not standing out in the open like everyone else? I tried to hurry us out the door, but Charles stopped me. He wanted to know why I had only invited him up to the newsroom once. I had truly never thought about it, since he usually came to my office at the end of the day to meet me for dinner or a show. I *had* given him a tour of the newsroom and introduced him to my favorite colleagues. Did he think I was ashamed of him? Perhaps that was why he was standing behind that bust.

The night of our party, as Charles waited in the kitchen for my answer, I thought back to the incident and what it said about us. Then I looked at him, the actual man in my life, and I realized that in the ways that truly mattered, he could be my ideal. He did not wear fancy clothes or have a lot of money, but what he had he happily shared with me. He was not the sort of man to make his views known during a dinner party, but his art spoke loudly about the way he viewed the world. Through his drawings it was obvious that he loved God and children and history and rainstorms and me.

"Charles," I said softly, when I went back into the kitchen. "Yes, it would be my honor to be your girlfriend."

He grinned and hugged me.

"Let's not pretend this is always going to be easy," I said. "Our lives are very different, and I don't want to give up my career to follow you around military bases. Can you handle that?"

"Dana, I'd never ask you to give up your career," he said. "We'll work it out."

We kissed, breathlessly, until the doorbell announced the arrival of our first guests.

That weekend was a turning point. The last of our guests lingered until after midnight, as Charles sat patiently on the couch stroking my hair. When we finally closed the door behind them, he pulled me into his arms and said that he loved me. He had been patient, but I knew he wanted to show me.

I was suddenly nervous and pulled away from him to change out of my low-cut blouse and black slacks. I returned wearing an oversize sweat suit and socks but was getting so worked up that I had begun to perspire. So I did an about-face and changed into a peach nightgown that fell below the knee but had spaghetti straps and a touch of lace at the décolletage. I walked back into the living room and asked Charles if he would like a beer. He did not have time to answer before I raced back into the bedroom and changed a third time, into my favorite nightshirt—a white oversize T-shirt with a picture of Mr. Potato Head that said: "The Perfect Boyfriend: He's cute, he's a good listener, and if he looks at another girl you can rearrange his face." The shirt fell just above my knees but it was not, unlike the nightgown, a neon sign flashing "Sexy."

Charles burst out laughing. "What are you trying to tell me?"

I was not sure whether he was talking about the message on my shirt or all the times I had changed, but I did not think it was the least bit funny. I paced the room, willing him not to notice my curves. I talked but do not remember what on earth about. Charles simply followed my movements with his eyes, clearly waiting for me to decide what would come next.

Then he stood up and walked slowly toward me. I was not used to seeing him so sure of himself, and it only increased my anxiety.

"What do you want?" he calmly asked, turning me to face him.

I was at once frightened and exhilarated. What if he hated my body? What if we made love and I lost control? Did this mean that I loved him?

No, he had not read his way through the *New York Times* best-seller list, but he could make me blush just by looking at me, and I could no longer fight my attraction. I had spent my life trying to control my emotions, but I had been hurt anyway. I was not nearly as tough as I pretended to be. I wanted somebody to hold, some-body who would *stay*. Perhaps I had found him in this gentle soul now gazing at me and waiting for my answer.

I put my hands on his chest and looked up at him.

"I want you," I said, and he gave me all of himself.

Five

Dear Jordan,

By the time your father came into my life, I had been dating long enough to know how to flirt and to put together a sexy outfit (usually black) to attract a man. What I still had not learned was how to fully love a man—or to let him love me. So when Charles turned to me a year into our relationship and said that he could see me being his wife someday, I panicked. We had settled into a rhythm that I was comfortable with and suddenly he wanted to change the tempo. I had given him space in my closet—no small thing in a city where every centimeter is precious. The doorman no longer stopped him on his way up to my apartment. Charles and I spent vacations together and most holidays. Our parents and siblings knew one another. Wasn't that commitment enough?

I loved Charles deeply and did not want to lose him, but I was still cynical about men and love and marriage. Perhaps it was because, when it came to understanding relationships, the only example I had was my parents', if that even counted.

Then, too, the question of our differentness had never gone away. Charles was a proud, traditional man. Although he expected his partner to contribute substantially he had always envisioned himself as the primary breadwinner.

*What makes a boy a man? When he has reached
maturity and fully understands what adult
responsibilities are required. What I mean is working,
paying bills, and being accountable for what you do.
Being a productive citizen in your environment and a
rock in your family, that is what's expected of you, son.*

I wondered if Charles could truly be happy married to a willful woman who earned considerably more than he did. I also wondered whether our marriage would survive if we lived in separate cities until he retired from the military. Charles was forty-one and intended to remain in the military at least another ten years. His goal was to attain the rank of sergeant major before retiring with a full pension and joining me in New York. Since I was seven years younger, he understood that I would be working long after he retired. But he worried that his pension would not go far in such an expensive city, and that he would not be able to contribute much toward a mortgage or other shared expenses. I pointed out that in New York he could pursue an art career, and he mentioned the possibility of working as a corporate security consultant or possibly a teacher.

I thought about all the changes Charles was willing to make to be with me and realized I had not even considered what sacrifices I would make for him. What if his daughter wanted to live with us? I had not seriously thought about what it meant to be a wife, let alone a stepmother. And what about children of our own? Charles had always wanted more kids, but I was still not sure I wanted any. I liked my independence too much—and my sleep.

Then I took stock of all that was good between me and Charles.

We had reached a point in our courtship where we knew things about each other that only come with time: shoe sizes, savings account balances, food allergies. I knew how to touch him when I was tired and wanted to quicken our lovemaking. He knew how to make me relax and get lost in the moment. I depended on him.

The trouble was, it was becoming difficult to make time for each other. We still talked on the phone every evening when neither of us was traveling, and we looked for ways to keep our passion from fading. Once he gave me an erotic drawing he had created of the two of us; I sent him cards with lipstick-stain kisses. But our jobs were increasingly demanding, and, between holidays, we spent months apart. Charles had been promoted again and was often out of contact during training exercises, which could be dangerous.

> *We were on maneuvers in Fort Riley, Kansas. I was a tank platoon sergeant. I had my platoon out conducting tank drills. It had been raining so the ground was pretty soft. I told my driver to drive through a ditch. Somehow the tank started leaning over to the right and finally it was on its side. I had a choice to give up, shut the tank off, or continue moving on. I told the driver to keep driving when the mud and soft ground caused the tank to level out. I looked down inside the tank to see how everyone was doing. They were just as frightened as I was. I didn't let them know, just laughed it off.*

Charles told me about this incident not long after it happened, explaining that if a tank rolled over, the occupants were often crushed. But I somehow knew there were other incidents I never heard about.

My job was not dangerous but, like Charles, I was intensely focused on my work. The *Times*'s top editors had chosen me in the summer of 1999 to participate in an ambitious project: a series of articles about race relations in America. I would be writing one of the stories as well as serving as one of the editors of the overall project. We would have a year to work exclusively on the series, and only the best stories would make it into the paper. I knew there was no way my career would survive if I spent a year writing one story and it was rejected for publication. The challenge consumed me.

I asked Charles to be patient until I finished the race project, as I was too distracted to make any life-altering decisions. He was supportive, but I was not sure he completely understood why I was still so driven after already having made it to the *Times*. He did not realize that I was still trying to demonstrate that I belonged, especially to those colleagues who considered the trainee program an affirmative-action scheme. Also, because of the high cost of living in New York, I had practically no money in the bank. If I could not succeed on my own, I had no one to fall back on financially.

The story I was writing was about two columnists for the *Akron Beacon Journal* in Ohio who had been major contributors to that newspaper's own series on race relations five years earlier. The series had won a Pulitzer, but, ironically, the paper had been beset by racial tension ever since. The columnists—one black, one white—had wrangled in print over the use of the word *niggardly*, and the debate had polarized the newsroom along racial lines. I was to spend that year following the men and interviewing their colleagues, bosses, and families to understand and chronicle what had been stirred up. That meant spending part of the week in Akron, then returning to New York to be part of the editing team.

By the fall, I was several months into the project and was overwhelmed and exhausted. I was living on airport and hotel food, had developed a persistent cough, and rarely got out of bed on the weekends. Charles tried to keep me focused. "I'm proud of you, girl!" he would say. "Keep doing your thing."

But we had not seen each other in a month, and I missed his touch.

"Charles, I need to be with you," I told him one bleak night, calling from yet another hotel room. He said he missed me, too, and that he would request a four-day pass as soon as possible. We agreed that we would stay in Akron and drive to Cleveland to surprise his parents, who hadn't seen him in months.

On a gray Friday afternoon, I was conducting interviews in the *Beacon Journal* newsroom, but my mind was on my man. He would be arriving in Akron that evening and taking a cab to my hotel. I could not wait to feel his breath on my neck and explore the ripples of muscle on his stomach.

By the time I got back to the hotel that October evening, the sky was overcast and the temperature had dropped precipitously. I opened a bottle of wine and poured myself a glass. Charles would be arriving in an hour, plenty of time to take a long shower, slather myself with scented lotion, and put on the black silk nightgown I had packed. But two and a half hours later, I had still not heard from Charles.

I tried his cell phone. No answer. I tried his parents and one of his friends. Again, no answer. I began to pace, feeling sick to my stomach. I turned on CNN to see whether there was news of a plane crash. I drank another glass of wine. Finally, I called the airline and confirmed that his plane had arrived safely, and on time.

At that point I knew Charles must have missed his flight. He had cut it close so many times before by staying at work too long. I also knew that rather than call and tell me the news, he might not phone at all. The thought infuriated me. I wanted to hear from him why he had been delayed. He could not possibly think I would have stayed the weekend in dreary, industrial Akron if I were not waiting for him. I wanted an explanation, and his silence struck me as monumentally selfish.

By midnight I had drunk most of the bottle of wine. I fell into an anxious sleep.

The ringing phone woke me in the middle of the night.

"Charles?" I said.

"Yeah." He sounded weary.

"Where are you?"

"Kansas," he said. "One of my soldiers' wives was having a baby and I had to go to the hospital to help him out."

"Help him do what?"

"Dana, he's just a kid. He was scared. Can we talk in the morning?" he pleaded.

"Are you kidding me?" I said, my voice rising. "First of all, it is nearly morning! Second, I'm stuck in Akron, Ohio, waiting for you, and you didn't even have the decency to call to let me know you weren't coming. I thought you were in a plane crash. Hell no, we're not waiting until the morning. I want to talk now."

The conversation deteriorated from there.

"Dana, you don't understand. I have to be there for my soldiers," Charles insisted.

Oh, I had heard all this before and had tried so hard to understand. I knew that he needed to be needed, to be a giver. He thrived on his paternalism. Caretaking—of me and his men—gave him a sense of purpose. But at that moment the balance seemed way off.

"Charles, I respect your dedication to your soldiers, I really do," I told him. "But I don't always agree with your priorities. It's one thing to be there to bail a guy out of jail or to help with a family emergency. It's another to give up what little time off you have to sit in a hospital holding a grown man's hand while his wife gives birth. That is not your job. We haven't spent any time together in almost six weeks, and then you don't show up over something like this."

There was a pause. Neither of us knew what to say.

"Are you coming tomorrow?" I finally asked.

He sighed. "No. I can't change my ticket, and I wouldn't be able to get there until late tomorrow afternoon anyway."

"Charles, I don't think you understand how hurt I am. We needed this time together, but if that wasn't going to happen you could have at least let me know. I could have taken a flight to come see you or gone home."

He was silent.

"Well, say something, Charles. What were you thinking?"

"I don't know."

"That's not good enough," I insisted. "Are you seeing another woman? Is that really why you missed your flight?" I knew it was a mistake to say it, but I was frustrated—and I had grown up with a father who always had flimsy excuses for his absences.

"Dana, of course not. You can talk to my soldier if you want to."

"I'm sure you could get any one of your soldiers to say anything you wanted."

"Dana, if you don't trust me by now, I don't know what to tell you. Have I given you any reason to think I'm cheating on you? You know where I am twenty-four hours a day."

"I didn't know where you were tonight," I shot back. "Then you have the nerve to call after midnight and expect me to accept your excuse. You let me sit here knowing I was going to be worried."

"I don't know what to tell you, Dana."

"Damn it, Charles, stop saying that. If we can't communicate any better than this and protect what little time we have together, then maybe this won't work." I paused, then said in anger, "I think maybe we should see other people."

Silence again.

"Fine, Dana, if that's what you want."

We said good-bye and hung up.

I sat on the edge of the bed, shaking and crying. I could not stop thinking about everything that had ever frustrated me about Charles: his passivity, his occasional jealousy, the way he sulked or shut down when he was upset. Even though I had gotten pretty good at it, I was tired of trying to read his mind.

I cried myself to sleep and awoke a few hours later to arrange a flight home. I sat by a window in my hotel room, watching the rain, and it was all I could do to choke down breakfast. I had to be back in Akron on Monday, but I needed to go home and tend to my wounds, if only for one night. I packed my bags in slow motion, hoping Charles would call, but the phone did not ring.

When the plane touched down at LaGuardia, the sky was overcast, but at least it was not raining. I sat in the cab with my head tilted back and my eyes closed, trying not to cry. I was still angry, but I missed Charles and did not know what to do.

The ache in my stomach returned when I got home and saw that he had not left a message. I took a shower, got into bed, and pulled the covers over my head.

The weekend went by and Charles still had not called. Then another week came and went with no word from him. I knew I had been wrong to suggest ending our relationship, but he was just as wrong for not arguing back—for giving up on us. And so easily. Charles knew the things I feared most were infidelity and rejection, and his leaving me in that hotel alone had fed my insecurities. I realized that he must be hurting, too, and that it was his dislike of conflict that made him clam up, but I still could not bring myself to call him.

We were at an impasse.

The week of silence turned into two and then three. This was the first real test of our relationship and we were failing. I gathered Charles's clothes, drawing pad, protein powder, and other belongings and put them in a box at the back of my closet. But I could not bring myself to send them to him. I could not believe that after all we had said that we meant to each other, we had not fought to hold on to what we had. I guess distance had made it too easy for us to avoid dealing with our differences.

Perhaps he was feeling sentimental as the holidays approached, because Charles finally called one evening in early November and said he missed me. He asked how the race project was going. I told him that we were making good progress but that I would be glad when it was over and I could take some time off. The conversation was polite but strained. There was so much I wanted to know. Why hadn't he called before now? Had he been dating? Did he still love me? I suspected that Charles had questions for me, too.

"Listen, Charles. I'm sorry about what happened. I know this is not the time, but I'd like to talk about it."

"Me, too," he said, and then surprised me. "Can I come see you?"

Surprising myself I said yes.

Charles arrived on a Friday evening a couple of weeks later. When I opened the door and saw him standing there, I put my arms around him and held on. He was bashful when I finally let go and he chuckled nervously. He took a seat on my chaise lounge and I asked if he was hungry. He said he was not and then stared at my apartment, as though seeking clues to my life without him. I sat next to him sipping a cup of tea. The awkwardness was painful. I decided to try to break through it.

"Charles, do you still care about me?"

He looked aghast.

"Of course, girl. Why do you think I'm here?"

I smiled and squeezed his arm.

"You know we have to talk about what happened, why our relationship was so fragile," I said.

He said he knew, but that we had all weekend. It did not take that long.

He followed me to the bedroom and I laid my head on his chest and fell asleep. Charles was staring at me when I awoke later that evening. He stroked my face and smiled.

"Did you sleep good?" he asked.

Sleep *well,* I almost corrected him, but caught myself. We still had not kissed, but lying in his arms felt right. We were finally relaxed enough to talk.

"So what happened? Why didn't you call me?" I asked softly, searching his face.

"I didn't know what to say, and I was upset that you didn't believe me and thought I was cheating on you."

I said that I was disappointed in us both. "I can't believe we gave up on us so easily. Does that mean it wasn't as real as we thought it was?"

He shifted his weight and stroked my hair again. He said he didn't know.

"Listen, we have to be able to talk. I know it's not easy for you, but I'm a communicator and I get really frustrated when you shut down."

"Well, I don't know what to say. But I still love you."

"I love you, too," I told him. "I know what happened was my fault, too, but we can't have a relationship if we can't talk, especially because of the distance between us. Sometimes talking is all we have, and we have to hold on until we can be together again."

"Are you saying you still want to be with me?" he asked.

I was scared. I was not about to leave my job, so I wondered how we would cope if he got stationed in Germany or Hawaii. Until then, all my serious relationships had been long-distance; I had literally kept men from getting too close. But I did not want to end up alone, and the time had come to let go of the pain I had carried around since childhood. There was no reason to believe that I was fated to be like my mother. Not every wife was so submissive, and most husbands did not have a second life with another woman.

Our time apart had also forced me to be honest about something else. Charles's love for me had been so intense that I had taken it for granted; I had not entirely opened up my heart to him. After all that time I had still not let go of that ideal imaginary man.

Now I realized that Charles *was* my ideal man. He was strong and kind and humble. He had the most character of anyone I had ever known and was the best judge of it in others. He considered it just as much his responsibility as mine to make our bed and scrub the bathroom. He was also the only man who had ever made me feel beautiful and protected. I loved his voice and his laugh and the way he walked. Most of all, I loved the little ways he loved me.

Once I had a suit-wearing, big-salary boyfriend who hated sharing his food and recoiled if I ate from his plate. Charles was the opposite: the more he enjoyed a meal, the more of it he fed to me.

Charles's heart was as big as his biceps, and even though I still found it irritating when he mispronounced a word, I had grown to love his mind. He could create landscapes from dots of ink but could also plot a battlefield on a computer. He quoted extensively from the Bible and began each day in prayer, but he could accept a woman who had not yet found her spiritual center.

I thought back to all the times I had said I loved him and realized that it was usually in response to his having said it first. He deserved better.

"Yes," I told Charles as he lay beside me. "I want you back in my life if you still want me. I love you so much."

He smiled broadly and then kissed me deeply.

"Crazy woman," he said. "I love you, too."

Well, son, Mom has gone through some changes and I love her just the way she is. I have not been able to be away from her too long. I pray now that I can always be with her.

I realized that day that our relationship would never be perfect. Only perfect for us.

Six

Dear Jordan,

On December 31, 1999, the taste of champagne still on our lips, your father and I stood in Times Square and kissed through the change of the year, the decade, the century, the millennium. I could never have imagined that, in the year to come, I would find myself in Florida in the middle of the unprecedented election melee that ultimately put George W. Bush in the White House; that September 11 would follow so swiftly; and that the man I dreamed of spending the rest of my life with would one day be sent to Iraq to help fight "the war on terror."

There we were that New Year's Eve, in each other's arms, confetti streaming around us—such a wildly romantic beginning of the end.

The *Times* published the race series in the summer of 2000, and in the fall I was promoted to national bureau chief in charge of news coverage for the state of Florida—a reward for my work on the project. That meant moving to Miami, a great news town and not a bad city to hang out in for a few years, I thought. True, Florida was farther from Kansas, where your father was still stationed, but by then we were used to jetting back and forth.

The plan was for me to move on Election Day 2000 and spend

a week or so settling in before I began my new assignment. Charles would visit as soon as I got my bearings. Those plans changed just hours after my plane touched down in Miami on November 7. I watched the seesawing Florida vote count from my hotel room in disbelief. By the time I went to sleep well after midnight, this peculiar election was still not over. It was the story of a lifetime, and I knew that there would be no phasing into my new job.

Day broke with a glorious streak of sherbet-orange sunlight stretched across the Atlantic. I longed to walk on the beach and savor it, but there was no time: the *Times* was flying in a team of political reporters from the Washington bureau. I sent an intern to my new apartment to meet the movers and went about trying to assess the magnitude of the election meltdown.

It was apparent within hours that the problems were widespread and that no one was in control. Ballots were missing in several cities, registered voters were turned away at the polls in some precincts, and there were claims of rigged results in others. The story I filed that day was the first of dozens of dispatches I wrote from around the state.

The pace of the work was grueling; I ran from news conferences to court hearings to voter protests. Elections officials in one county would halt ballot recounts only to be ordered by a judge to resume. Another county would proclaim its counting complete and then discover more uncounted ballots.

There was nothing like having a front-row seat while history was being made. I was nearly trampled outside the Miami County Board of Elections office when someone mistakenly thought a Democratic official had slipped a ballot into his pocket and dozens of Republican operatives and Democratic strategists began shoving one another. Less dramatic but far more troubling were the young people I spent a day interviewing. They had voted for the first time and now wondered whether their ballots had been counted. I felt so sad for them that their first experience at the polls had been marked by doubt and confusion rather than the pride I had felt when I voted for the first time.

My colleagues and I put our personal lives on hold. About three weeks into the recount, some of us discovered that we had run out of clean clothes and stopped into a store to buy socks and underwear. My boxes were still packed, and on the rare evening I was home before ten I had neither the time nor the energy to rip them open in search of my microwave oven or pots and pans to cook. Over dinner at a restaurant late one night, a reporter from Chicago said he had tried to call home for his messages and discovered that his phone had been disconnected because he had not had time to pay his bills. One of my colleagues had run out of prescription medication and decided to do without it until the story ended. Another was driving with an out-of-state license that had just expired.

We all worked well past midnight every day and did not stop until, five weeks after Election Day, the United States Supreme Court declared President George W. Bush the winner.

"Well, you said you wanted a challenge," Charles reminded me in one of our few conversations during those hectic days.

I told him that I could not believe I was bearing witness to events that our grandchildren would one day be studying in history class.

"I mean that metaphorically," I added quickly, "not that we're necessarily going to have grandchildren together."

"I know what you meant," he said.

By the spring of 2001, not only had I survived the Florida recount, but the race project had been chosen as a finalist for a Pulitzer Prize. I flew to New York that April to stand among my colleagues when the judges announced the winners. As we waited in the *Times* newsroom, I struggled to contain my emotions. There was a time when someone who looked like me—black and a woman—would have only been in that spot if she were emptying a wastebasket. I thought about my grandmother, Everlener Canedy, who was forced to drop out of school in the seventh grade and work as a domestic in order to support her brothers and sisters after her father died and her mother became gravely ill. She could read little more than birthday cards and traffic signs, but she could recognize my name, and she loved to see my byline.

Through a fog I heard these words: "The prize for public service goes to the *New York Times,* for 'How Race Is Lived in America.'"

Someone handed me a glass of champagne. There was hugging, shouting, more champagne. The executive editor made a speech I did not hear as I picked up a phone and left a message for Charles.

"Sweetie, we won!" I shouted into the receiver. "I wish you were here."

When I finally reached Charles late that night, I reminded him that the Pulitzer project was a team effort, but that was picking nits to him.

> *Did you know that your mom received a Pulitzer Prize for working on a race project? You would never know it by talking to her. She is really modest about her accomplishments and her profession. I admire her no-fear work ethic. I learned from your mother that the sky is the limit and you are just as good as anyone else. She has shown me that with hard work and determination you can succeed.*

The times we saw each other were blessed respites from our exhausting work lives. Charles spent long weekends with me in Florida, since his living arrangements tended to be sparse and he liked escaping to Miami. We danced salsa, or tried to, at Latin clubs on Ocean Drive, watched elderly Cuban men in guayaberas roll cigars in Little Havana, and awoke to see dolphins splashing in the bay outside my bedroom window.

We also took cruises to the Caribbean and made love in cabins with tiny beds, turquoise water flashing through the porthole. Charles would stretch out in a deck chair and sip rum punch to the sounds of a calypso band. In Puerto Rico, we kissed greedily at sunset on the beach. Once, on a ship with a rink, I convinced Charles to go rollerblading—the only thing besides dancing that he was bad at.

At each port your father insisted on sticking a camera in my face, and each time I protested that the camera added ten pounds and asked him to stop. He would smile and keep snapping.

You'll see all the photos of your mother and me, all of the different places we have journeyed. Now that we have you they mean so much more. I hope that you treasure and enjoy them. Love, Dad.

As much as we cherished those interludes, Charles and I were old enough to realize that real love could not survive on picnics in a kayak and weekend getaways to the Florida Keys. There would come a time when we would finally live together and contend with each other's laundry and bouts of flu. I wondered how we would handle the change.

Then came September 11.

I was in Miami covering a campaign appearance that dreadful day. Janet Reno, the attorney general during the Clinton administration, was running for governor in her home state against incumbent Jeb Bush. Ms. Reno was appearing at a senior citizens center and was running late, which was unusual for her. She finally arrived, looking grave—also unusual for a woman who enjoyed campaigning so much that she traveled the state in a red pickup truck to meet voters. Two planes had just struck the World Trade Center towers and the Pentagon was on fire, Ms. Reno announced. The United States was under attack. I stood there writing what she was saying in a notebook and then abruptly stopped. I was worried about my colleagues and friends in New York. And Janet Reno's campaign was no longer news.

I ran to my car and turned on the radio. A commercial plane was in pieces in a Pennsylvania field. I called Charles in Kansas and told him to turn on his television. The cable news stations were broadcasting an almost continuous loop of footage of a plane slicing into one of the towers.

"Oh, man," Charles said. Then he spoke the words I was afraid to say aloud. "We're going to war with somebody."

I drove back to the office with the radio on, listening in horror as the towers, one after another, collapsed. I was terrified of this unknown enemy who hated America so fiercely. I thought of all the people who had probably just died in the attacks and said a silent prayer for their souls.

We're going to war with somebody. I dismissed a nagging thought about whether your father might eventually be called upon to respond to the attacks. My immediate concern was for the people I loved in New York, especially my colleagues at the paper. I knew that many of them had likely headed into danger to report the news.

The thing about journalists is that we often live life backwards. We fly into hurricanes, arrive at buildings that are being evacuated, race to crime scenes while bullets are still flying. It can be grim work, but most of us consider it a calling. Now I needed to know whether my colleagues were safe, but all telephone circuits into New York City were busy. Instead, I reached several of my fellow bureau chiefs in cities across the country. We had a conference call to discuss how we could best help with the coverage. I set about tracking down local and state officials to assess the situation in my state. What was Miami doing to secure its ports? Had Disney World and other theme parks been evacuated? Had the governor heard from his brother, the president, who had been in the state reading to schoolchildren when he heard that the country was under attack?

My contribution to the next day's newspaper was minimal, but I would soon have much more responsibility. Within days, federal law enforcement officials announced that the terrorists had trained at flight schools in Florida. It was time to dig in for my second big assignment in just over a year.

I tracked down flight instructors who had trained the attackers and neighbors who had had no idea who they really were. I stood in the hotel room where two of the hijackers had stayed the night before the attacks. The remains of a boxed Indian meal were in the wastebasket; the checkout date on their hotel registration card was September 11. I visited the restaurant where a bartender told me that two of the hijackers drank vodka and rum for three straight hours the night before the attacks and then seemed reluctant to pay their forty-eight-dollar tab.

For months I was under tremendous pressure to report new developments—a daunting task because every major newspaper and television network was aggressively covering the story. Being relatively new to the city, I also did not have many sources in the police department and the local FBI office to leak me information. I managed to hold my own, but the story was much harder to cover than the election had been.

At about this time, your father was hand-selected by the Defense Department for a new assignment reserved for the military's most elite personnel. He moved to Fort Irwin, California, in January 2002 to be part of a team that evaluated troops for combat readiness at the army's National Training Center. The military had built a billion-dollar simulated Iraq deep in the Mojave Desert, complete with mock operating bases and Iraqi villages, in which Iraq's exiles acted as civilians and insurgents. Charles's job was to observe recruits as they conducted simulated assaults and gauge their proficiency with weapons and familiarity with combat rules of engagement. The exercises kept him in the field for more than a month at a time, but Charles saw it as a grave responsibility: The training might one day save the life of a young man or woman who less than a year earlier had been taking their sweetheart to the prom, or that of a career soldier close to retirement.

This marked the second time since I had arrived in Florida that your father and I were forced to put our jobs before our relationship. This time, the long stints apart were taking a toll on us. Our conversations had become brief and perfunctory. We sometimes forgot to say we loved each other when we hung up. I considered asking for a transfer to the Los Angeles bureau to be closer to Charles. Then I realized that he might simply get orders for a new posting after I relocated. So we made do with whatever time we could find to be together.

Just before Charles began his job in Fort Irwin, we decided to spend two weeks reconnecting on a cruise from Miami to the Caribbean. We set sail on a sunny Thursday evening and woke up the next morning in Key West. I ate conch fritters for brunch and Charles drank coconut milk from a shell. On the second day I suggested we test our skills on the ship's two-story rock climbing wall. Big mistake. I only made it halfway up the wall and then could not raise my arms above my chest for three days.

> *We were on a cruise where I let your mother talk me into rock climbing. We were so sore. Earlier that day, I went walking through the ship mall to buy something for your mom. I was walking by a spa when I decided to get a spa package with the massage bath and regular massage. She loved it so much. She still talks about it today.*

The day after our rock climbing expedition, the cruise director made an announcement about diamond wholesalers at the next port, in Cozumel. Charles suggested that we visit them to look at rings. He had told me years earlier that my reaction when he asked me to be his girlfriend hurt him so much that he would never attempt a surprise marriage proposal. So I suspected that this was his way of trying to determine how receptive I was to the idea of becoming his wife.

"Are you suggesting we get engaged?" I asked.

He admitted that he had been thinking about it. He said he had been lonely lately and wanted to have a family again. I was glad to know that he still loved me so much after our lengthy separation and agreed to go to the jeweler, but hastily added that we should not feel pressured to buy a diamond, duty-free or not.

The diamond district was a glitzy strip of shops offering

complimentary champagne and a free setting with every stone. We walked into a store and a salesman congratulated us heartily. I wanted to say that we hadn't yet decided anything, but that seemed rude. I perched on a stool, with Charles beside me, while the salesman laid out a black velvet tray. He asked what size stone we were looking for. Charles was silent.

"I, we don't know," I stammered.

The truth was, I felt unprepared for marriage. And why make it official now? We could scarcely find time to be together. Since my job enabled me to move back to New York when I wanted, my hope was that Charles would eventually be the one to arrange for a transfer, perhaps to a base near the city. We could make the decision then. There was just so much that we had never discussed, like the fact that marrying him would mean giving up any hopes of someday becoming a foreign correspondent and moving to a different part of the world. Charles had been through one divorce already, and I had seen how it had torn him up. I did not want someday to be the cause of such heartache.

Now here I was sliding rings on my finger and holding them up to the light. Charles watched and adjusted his baseball cap. I could not read his expression. Was he thinking the stones were too big or was he sorry that he had suggested the trip to the jeweler in the first place?

"They're all beautiful, but I need some air," I said, returning a ring to the tray and grabbing Charles's hand. As soon as we had made our escape, I hugged him, kissed his cheek, and whispered, "I love you so much, but let's not do this today."

"Come on, you crazy woman," he said, good-naturedly—which surprised me, given the risk that he had taken in bringing me to that store. "Let's go to the beach."

At dinner that night, I told Charles that I didn't want us to be one of those couples that rush into marriage because of the grief of 9/11. We had so much time, I told him.

"You've been an independent woman a long time," he said. "Are you sure you want to get married at all?"

"Charles, listen to me," I said, taking his hands in mine. "I love you and I do want to marry you, eventually. But we've never even lived in the same city. Doesn't that concern you?"

"No, I know you, Dana."

"But, Charles, we haven't really discussed what we expect from marriage."

He said he did not expect much. "I just want to be your king and make you my queen."

"That sounds nice," I said, "but what does that *mean*? Would you expect me to come home from work every day and cook you dinner? Would you care if I didn't take your last name?"

"I don't care about you cooking or what name you call yourself," he said.

It was a good start—but, to my mind, only a beginning.

We turned our attention to our food and I convinced Charles to try escargots. To his surprise, he liked them and ate the entire appetizer. The gentle swaying of the ship soothed me and I wanted to be in his arms. We finished our dinner and went to the lido deck to indulge in a late-night chocolate buffet and music under the stars. We danced slow and close in the moonlight and breathed in the sea air between kisses.

Then all too soon our two weeks together were over. Except for an occasional weekend getaway, we spent the rest of winter and most of the spring apart, as his number of combat-readiness missions suddenly increased. He never complained, but I knew he was tired of being in the desert and sleeping alone. He said when the temperature dipped at night, he imagined my warm body next to his.

I was simply grateful that, as a troop instructor, Charles could not be deployed to Afghanistan. It might be scorching by day and cold at night in the California desert, but at least he was not atop a mountain in the Middle East searching in the darkness for Osama bin Laden. There were times when Charles hinted that he felt uneasy being involved in mock battles when so many soldiers were fighting the real fight. I reminded him that he had already served several combat missions and that the training he was overseeing was vital.

One day in late spring, Charles told me that he was going to take a few days off so that we could spend our birthdays together. But with so many soldiers he knew being deployed to Afghanistan, he was in no mood for grand getaways. We would spend our time in Miami, but I was determined to make it as festive as possible. I spent a week searching for a gift for him before settling on a handsome set of Italian leather luggage. The only suitcases he owned looked as though they were held together with duct tape, but I knew that it would not occur to him to replace them.

The day he arrived, I left the office early and came home carrying a large box wrapped in bright gift paper. He met me at the door, smiling. I set down the box and he wrapped me in a long embrace.

"I missed you," he said.

I felt like a little girl ready to blow out candles and hand out party favors. I couldn't wait to see his face when he unwrapped my gift, and I have to admit that I couldn't wait to see what he had chosen for me. But as soon as he noticed my box, he looked panic-stricken.

"Let's open our gifts now," I said excitedly. He stammered and continued to eye the box nervously as I handed it to him.

"Do you like it?" I asked, beaming, when he tore off the tissue paper covering the black leather and pulled out one of the pieces.

"Wow," he said, looking stunned. He studied each piece of luggage before slowly returning them to the box. Then he got up and paced nervously. He seemed to be stalling.

"I have something for you, too," he finally said. "But it's not much."

He handed me something the size of a small book, and I tore off the wrapping paper. It was a paperback novel. I wrinkled my forehead in confusion.

"I know how much you like to read," he said, weakly.

"Charles, don't try that," I snapped. "You forgot to get me a gift, didn't you? I'm not stupid. You picked this up in the airport."

"Look, honey, I've been busy. I'm sorry. I just wanted to make the flight."

I was fuming, and we barely spoke that evening or before I left for work the next morning. When I got home that evening, there was a tiny jewelry box on the coffee table. Charles was nervous, I could see, as I ripped off the pretty paper and opened the box. Inside was a delicate pair of gold hoop earrings. There was a problem, though. Try as I might, I could not fasten them around my earlobes.

"Great, Charles. First you forget my gift altogether, and now you've managed to get me something that makes me feel like even my ears are fat!" I chided, only half-joking.

He was crestfallen. We drove back to the store together to return the earrings, Charles rubbing his temples, me huffing. I explained the problem to the sales clerk as Charles leaned on the counter, looking wounded.

"Ma'am," the salesman said, "these earrings are for babies."

Charles and I burst out laughing.

With all that had been going on in the world, it felt good to laugh about a fight over something as frivolous as birthday presents. I was glad, too, that Charles and I had reached a point in our relationship in which it could withstand a feud or two—and, believe me, we had them. I finally trusted him to stay.

I could be myself with Charles because he saw me as the woman I hoped to be instead of the one who was easily agitated, occasionally hypercritical, and always obsessing over a few extra pounds. I recalled how moved I had been by his devotion when he accompanied me to the National Association of Black Journalists' annual convention in Orlando the summer before. While I attended workshops and interviewed potential *Times* applicants, Charles sat by the pool drawing and catching up on his rest.

I had been asked to deliver a speech at the closing night banquet, and I rehearsed it every evening in our hotel room. Each time I made it to the end, Charles clapped and proclaimed the speech perfect. But I was nervous. I did not tell him that my anxiety had nothing to do with the speech but instead with the fact that my exboyfriend, Greg, and his new wife would be in the audience.

Charles did not want to put on a suit and make small talk with strangers while I sat on the dais, and I did not protest: by now I understood his shyness, and when he said he would rather stay behind and work on a drawing, I didn't mind. He was so grateful that he offered to iron my outfit. I chose a lavender blouse and a snug gray skirt—then changed my mind when I saw it on.

"It's too plain, and my hips look huge."

He pulled my red suit out of the closet.

"Too hot," I protested.

He ironed a silk fuchsia blouse with three-quarter-length sleeves for me to wear with a floor-length black satin skirt. I put it on and was doing a slow turn in the mirror when Charles walked up behind me and put his hands on my shoulders. He rubbed my back and then slowly turned me to face him.

"Dana," he said, "you're not Greg's girl anymore. You're a woman with a woman's body. You look beautiful. Now go give your speech."

I was astonished. How had he known?

I lowered my eyes in embarrassment. I had never felt so loved.

"I'm sorry," I said, just above a whisper. I kissed him deeply, reapplied my lipstick, and walked out feeling more confident than I had in a long while. And though I caught sight of Greg in the ballroom moments before I walked to the podium, the only man I was interested in impressing was my own.

Whether Charles was giving me a pep talk about facing my former boyfriend or laughing off my silliness about a birthday gift, he always made it clear that he was with me for the long haul. But we were living in a season of seismic shifts that kept shaking our foundation.

On the evening of March 19, 2003, President Bush addressed the nation and announced that the United States was declaring war on Iraq. "My fellow citizens, at this hour American and coalition forces are in the early stages of military operations to disarm Iraq, to free its people, and to defend the world from grave danger," the president said.

I would soon have a part in chronicling the war. After two and a half years as bureau chief, I was promoted to assignment editor for national news and moved back to New York. My job included assigning national reporters to track relatives of some of the soldiers in combat. The national desk was also responsible for periodic stories intended to gauge Americans' support of the war. When the military approached the terrible milestone of one thousand U.S. soldier deaths in 2004, I sent a team of reporters to cover some of the funerals and put names and faces to the "casualties of war," a term I hated. Those soldiers had mothers and children and names like Taylor and Diego—and Charles.

Charles and I did not discuss in any depth whether we thought the invasion and occupation of Iraq was right or wrong. We had our reasons: after 9/11, he would not have questioned his commander in chief, and, as a journalist for one of the world's most prominent newspapers, I was used to maintaining a posture of neutrality. Then, too, I suppressed what frightened me most— that he could be sent into combat. So I simply avoided talking about it.

Charles was promoted to the rank of first sergeant in June 2004 and reassigned to Fort Hood, Texas. There he was put in charge of an entire company, comprising more than one hundred soldiers. It was a great honor, but I did not meet the news with the same excitement that he did. It meant that he could now be deployed.

Less than six months into his new assignment, Charles called me with the news I had dreaded.

"Honey," he said softly, "I got orders for Iraq."

Seven

Dear Jordan,

Orders for Iraq. I heard the words your father spoke that winter day in 2004, but my mind would not accept them. He simply could not be sent into battle. It had taken us too long to find each other.

"Oh God, Charles, please don't tell me that," I said. And then: "Can't you get out of it?"

"No, Dana," he said gently. "I put on the uniform and I take the paycheck, so I have to go where the commander in chief sends me."

I knew that would be his answer as well as I knew that he was somehow relieved to be joining the war. For months he had felt guilty about preparing soldiers for a battle he was not himself fighting. To him, it was like violating a sacred oath. Nothing I said eased his torment, especially after he began to hear from buddies he had served with during the First Gulf War who were heading back to Iraq.

I could have begged or railed. I could have pleaded with Charles to consider how his elderly parents would react. I *did* have political views about the war—everyone did, and I could have forced him into debating the issue. But none of that seemed right now. What mattered was supporting my man. I certainly did not want to risk saying anything that would hurt his morale or make him question his mission.

"When will you go?" I asked.

"The end of next year," Charles said, and I thought I heard relief in his tone again. In the last few months, he had begun to reflect more and more on his time serving in Operation Desert Storm. Even knowing the dangers he would face, he felt his orders somehow completed him.

I found myself thinking of the past, too. When I had vowed years earlier never to marry a soldier, it was because I feared replicating painful parts of my childhood and limiting my career choices. I had never considered a far greater risk: that my man might be sent into battle.

It took Charles's pending deployment to throw everything else into perspective. The personal commitments that I had so long been afraid of I now wanted desperately. I loved being a journalist and as a reporter had considered it a point of pride that my editors knew I kept a packed suitcase in my car and my laptop nearby in case they needed an "unencumbered" reporter in a hurry. I had even achieved the financial security I sought, but I was also approaching forty. Hopping on a plane at a moment's notice was no longer a thrill. Waking up in a hotel and not remembering what city I was in no longer seemed like an adventure. On some level I must have known this; I had accepted the editing job in New York when I could have become a foreign correspondent or a national bureau chief in another city. Now I stayed in one place and sent other people to unfamiliar cities to cover wildfires and plane crashes. I wanted to experience more of life, not merely report on it.

One evening, when Charles called to tell me about his latest drawing, I was distracted and cut him off.

"I want to have a baby," I blurted out.

He thought I was joking and laughed.

"I'm serious, Charles. I want to try to get pregnant."

He was silent for a minute. "Why?"

The question lingered.

Charles knew that I had never particularly wanted children. I liked them well enough and adored my nieces and nephews, but I had seen so many parents struggle financially, including my own. I wanted the freedom to focus on my career without worrying about being a breadwinner and a nursemaid. I never had the baby lust that lots of women feel when they reach their thirties. I was too busy building up my 401(k), going on safari in South Africa, and standing by for the next assignment to Puerto Rico or the Dominican Republic. I had put off deciding about a child for so long that not having a family suddenly felt like a *default* choice— and I liked to have more control over my life than that.

Of course, the issue was not just my feelings; it was about whether Charles and I would be good parents together. So many children, African Americans especially, were growing up without fathers. Charles, I knew, would love me and any child of ours too much to ever leave us. He was the only man who had been patient enough to really try to understand me—and to love me anyway. I knew he would be an equally patient father.

I wanted to be his wife as well as the mother of his child, but I knew him well enough to know that he was too traditional to entertain a proposal from a woman. He needed to do the asking, in his time and in his way.

As I thought about how to answer Charles's immediate question, it occurred to me that he was not aware of something: the balance of power in our relationship had shifted. The days of him pursuing me and me letting him were over. I had urged him more than once during difficult moments in our relationship to date other people, but I was now thankful he had not found anyone to replace me. I loved him more than he knew, and it was time to make him see.

My answer to his question was definitive. I told him I had never known a man with such amazing character and strength and spirituality. I told him that he was my best friend, but that I had also never experienced such passion with a man.

I did not say that knowing that our baby was growing inside of me might sustain us both during the long year ahead.

"Do you think it's even possible?" Charles asked.

"All we can do is try," I said. "If you want to."

"Absolutely," he said, startling me with his certainty.

"Really, don't you want to think about it awhile? I'm not asking you for a puppy, you know."

"No, I don't need to think about it," Charles said emphatically.

"Are you sure?"

"Stop asking me that," he said. "You're the one who doesn't sound sure."

"It's just that I don't understand how you can make a decision like this so quickly," I said.

"I made it a long time ago," he said.

I reached into a drawer in my nightstand. "I'm about to throw out my birth control pills."

He said, "Go ahead."

Your mother and I had talked about having a baby and I immediately said yes. I realized how serious your mother was about the idea. We had been seeing each other off and on for nearly six years, maybe longer. I felt like she would be a great mother and she wanted to have a child before it was too late. We also wanted to have you in a timely manner because your mother knew I was going off to the war in Iraq December 1, 05.

That night I thought again about how well Charles had come to understand me, and how that helped me to better know myself. Once, when I came home from work furious about a disagreement with my boss, I followed Charles around the apartment, animatedly recounting what had happened. He did not say a word. Finally I turned to him and asked, "Well, don't you have any advice?" Barely pausing for an answer, I resumed my rant. When I was done, I realized that while I was talking he had drawn me a bubble bath, lit candles, and put on a jazz CD.

Wordlessly, he helped me undress and lowered me into the warm water. Then he handed me a glass of Chardonnay, set a bowl of popcorn beside me, and told me he was going for a walk. I was finally speechless. By the time he returned forty-five minutes later, I was watching a sitcom and laughing out loud. Charles might not have had much to say about office politics or the newspaper business, but he knew what I needed, sometimes better than I did.

Knowing he would rarely ask for anything for himself, I tried to anticipate his needs, too. I could tell from the way he moved when his muscles were sore and he needed a massage. If he got out of bed in the middle of the night to draw, I knew something was troubling him, and that if I sat quietly beside him long enough, he would tell me about it. I knew that he enjoyed long baths nearly as much as I did but would not take one unless I prepared it for him.

It would be two months before Charles's next break in training, but I could not contain my excitement about our decision. We had agreed not to tell anyone until there was something to say—but I went ahead and told my mother, my sisters, and my closest girlfriends.

"Girl, that's going to be a beautiful baby," said my friend Loretta.

"I'm not pregnant yet," I said.

"Yes, but when you put your mind to something, you usually do it," she said.

This was different. Charles's preparations were intensifying and his deployment was just months away. We would have only three or four weekends to try to conceive. I had no idea whether my childbearing years had already passed, and Charles and I decided that if we could not conceive, we would not pursue infertility treatments. If we were meant to create a life together, it would happen naturally. If it did not, we would try again after his tour of duty.

Charles was the only deeply religious man I had dated—a man so intoxicated with love for me that he compromised his traditional values to please me. I realized that he would have preferred that we get married before having a baby, but I also suspected that he somehow still thought asking for more of a commitment might frighten me away. He had grown accustomed to not knowing what to expect from me, and he did not want to risk losing our relationship—I had become his confessor and "earth angel." Imagine: an anxious, demanding earth angel. That is who I was, though, and Charles accepted it. He set aside his own desires to satisfy mine. So when he came to New York during a training break the last weekend in June, we clung to each other with an urgency I had never experienced, as though we were trying to will a baby into being.

As I lay there listening to Charles breathe in the dark that first night, I wondered, guiltily, about my own motives. Somewhere, amid the certainty of our love, the faith in Charles's commitment to fatherhood, and the desperate hope that a pregnancy would make it easier for us to endure our separation, there was a cold calculation: the odds were slim at my age of finding another man to father my child if he did not return alive from the war. Did Charles see that side of me, too?

At dinner the following night, Charles told me he had prayed a long time for us to be a family, and I was suddenly petrified. "But what if I'm not good at being a mother?" I asked him. "I've been focused on myself for so long. What if we have a baby and it hates me?"

Charles chuckled. Then he leaned back in his chair, folded his massive arms across his chest, and smiled.

"It's not funny," I said.

When he spoke again it was in as soft yet as steady a voice as I had ever heard from him. "You really have no idea how good you're going to be at this, do you?" he said.

Tears fell from my eyes. I realized then that I did not just want a baby—I wanted *his* baby. I leaned forward and kissed him.

"Do you think we should become an official family?" Charles asked.

"Are you asking me to marry you?"

"Yes," he said, lowering his head in anticipation, or maybe fear, of my answer.

Whatever part of me was still protecting those old wounds fell away. I felt healed. I said yes, and meant it with all my heart.

> *I wanted to be with your mother really bad and prayed about it because I wanted a family. She was not interested at first. I had pretty much given up the idea but she changed her mind. And by some miracle, she thought it would be great to have a son. It took a while but my prayers got answered.*
>
> *I still have a fire in my heart for her.*

Charles got up and knelt beside me. He kissed my hands and pulled me into his arms. It was time to go home, he said. We had only two more days together and spent most of the time in bed.

Four days later I suspected I was pregnant and went to my doctor to have the news confirmed. She asked how far along I thought I was.

"About four days," I said.

The doctor looked as though she felt sorry for me. I was clearly a desperate woman. But she went along with it and soon I was emptying my bladder into a plastic cup. I waited in an exam room while a nurse checked the results.

"Negative," the young woman said and left. I sat there for several minutes, agitated and in disbelief. I had been so sure.

Slowly, I made my way out onto the chaotic midtown streets. I needed to get back to work but kept walking instead. Your father was in the desert and would be out of touch for weeks, so I called my sister Lynnette in her office in Los Angeles.

"Hey, are you busy?" I asked, not waiting for a response. "I just left the doctor's office. I took a pregnancy test and it came back negative. I think it's wrong."

She reminded me that I was forty years old and had just started trying. "What are the chances you would get pregnant on the first try?" she said.

"I was just so sure."

In the days that followed, the test result nagged at me. Three times in as many days I walked into a drugstore, picked up a home pregnancy kit, and put it back on the shelf. I called my sister again to tell her that I was still convinced I was pregnant.

"Go ahead and spend the money on the test, so you'll have some peace."

I took her advice and went out immediately to buy a kit. Twenty minutes later I poured myself a vodka tonic to steady my nerves and went into my bathroom. I sipped my drink, then took the stick out of the box with shaking hands. But when I was done I could not bring myself to look at the results. I called Lynnette back.

"Go ahead," she said, cheering me on.

Two pink lines meant a positive result. And there were two— except the second line was very faint.

"Oh my God!" my sister yelled. "Go get another test!"

Two more kits and the same results, a clearly defined pink line and the hint of a second one. Lynnette told me to call the 800 number on the test box. Within minutes a recorded message gave me my answer.

Even a faint pink line meant the test was positive.

"Oh my God," I screamed. "I'm pregnant!"

Lynnette squealed and hung up to call my other sisters.

I picked up my drink and put it to my lips, then stopped and poured it down the drain. No more alcohol.

The doctor confirmed the results the next day. I was about two weeks pregnant. She congratulated me and said the first test had been taken too soon after I conceived to detect the pregnancy.

It was official. Hard as it was to believe, Charles and I had conceived on our first attempt.

He got back from the field two weeks later and called me at once. The training had not gone particularly well, he said. The nights in the desert were frigid, the days scorching, and he couldn't get the men to keep the heavy equipment on. "They were passing out and throwing up in the heat," he said. "But it's going to be even hotter in Iraq. I finally had to tell them that if I catch them without their gear when we get to Iraq, I'm going to dock their combat pay."

What he was saying was disturbing. Charles was in great shape, but it bothered me to think of him wearing hot, cumbersome equipment in Iraq. I reminded myself that he had been there before and survived.

"I know that if anybody can get those soldiers ready to go, it's you. You still have time," I said. "And by the way, sweetie, we missed you."

Charles went on talking. I asked whether he had heard what I said.

"No, what?"

"I said, 'We missed you.'"

"*Who* missed me?" Charles asked, bewildered.

"Both of us," I said, "I'm pregnant."

He laughed long and loud.

I was training at the National Training Center in Fort Irwin, Ca. for forty days when your mother found out. Trust me, I was in complete shock and disbelief when your mother told me she was pregnant. Thank you, God.

"Honey, are you sure? How are you feeling?"

"Yes, I'm sure, and I feel fine," I said. "I saved one of the little test sticks as a souvenir for you."

He laughed again, then turned serious.

"Dana, thank you."

"Don't thank me, Charles. Just be there when this baby is born and come home to help me raise it."

"I will," he promised.

Eight

Dear Jordan,

Before he left for Iraq, your father was preparing for two lives. One week he would be drilling his soldiers in the rules of engagement for confronting a lethal enemy, the next clutching my hand and staring in amazement at ultrasound images of you. How he coped with such incongruity—the peril and the promise—I will never know. There was little I could do to help him maintain his balance.

I tried to protect him any way I could, just as he tried to do the same for me. He said almost nothing about the missions he would lead. I never told him about those days in my first trimester when it looked as if your health might be in doubt.

Charles and I had always lived disparate lives, but now the distance between us seemed immense. At Fort Hood, he spent his mornings sharpening his shooting skills and studying maps of Iraq. I spent mine behind a desk shaping coverage of that day's news—when I was not bent over a toilet vomiting. It was only in the evenings that we had the chance to connect. In long phone conversations, we discussed baby names or the advice I had gleaned from my growing stack of prenatal books. I told Charles of my excitement the day the doctor calculated my due date, March 25,

2006, and about how I could not stop patting and rubbing my still relatively flat stomach. Charles asked how much weight I had gained, advised me to add more protein to my diet or to drink more water, and reminded me to take my prenatal vitamins. I had never answered to a man in my life, certainly not about my weight, but this intimacy felt right.

Still, we did have secrets, and keeping them was easy from a distance. I didn't mention the morning I became flushed and dizzy on the subway and ended up sitting against a filthy steel column in Grand Central Station, legs splayed out in front of me. Two police officers asked if I needed an ambulance. I managed to say that I was pregnant and just needed to rest a minute. I sucked on a few pieces of peppermint candy until I regained my energy and slowly made my way to the office. After a check of my blood pressure and a nap in the medical department, I had recovered enough to work the rest of the day.

Charles called that evening, just as I was drifting off to sleep.

"How are you feeling, Ma?" he asked, using the new nickname he had adopted when he found out I was expecting. (I secretly detested it, but he fell into it so easily, I didn't have the heart to tell him.)

"Fine, just tired. How was your day?"

"All right. Just busy."

We were working so hard to shield each other that it sometimes didn't leave much to say.

We established a routine. He began his workday at 5 a.m. and usually did not make it home before 9 p.m., when he would call to check on me while he ironed his uniform or ate, usually a ready-made salad and a steak or canned tuna. On weekends and the rare occasions when he left work by 7 p.m., we ate dinner while we talked on the phone and called it "family meal time." As my pregnancy progressed, I needed to eat earlier and it became more difficult to stay awake for our phone calls. At times, I fell asleep with Charles still talking. He would remain on the line listening to me breathe until he started to doze himself. The sound soothed him, he said, and was a nice end to his day.

"Even when I snore?"

"You purr," he said.

Except for the morning sickness and occasional dizziness, my first trimester went well until the evening in early August when I walked into my bedroom and doubled over with a pain so intense that it felt like my ovaries were on fire. I stumbled to the phone in a panic.

"I want you to go to the emergency room," my doctor said calmly. "I hope it's not an ectopic pregnancy."

I called my best friend, Miriam, crying hysterically, and asked between sobs for her to meet me at the hospital. She wanted to come get me, but I said it would be quicker to meet there. I knew that was the right call, but I had never felt more alone than on that cab ride to the hospital.

Miriam and I had birthdays only four days apart, and we joked that we were twins who were easy to distinguish because one was tall and black and the other short and white. She was the New York City bureau chief for the *Philadelphia Inquirer,* but we had met as interns and later cub reporters at the *Plain Dealer* in Cleveland and had been friends for almost twenty years. We knew most of each other's secrets and had seen each other through boyfriend blues, career calamities, and dieting dramas. Since she was a fellow Clevelander, Charles called her "homegirl," and we chose her to be your godmother. I loved having her so close, especially with your father so far away. But I had not expected to need her so much so soon.

When I lifted my head off the hospital pillow that night, still sobbing, and saw Miriam standing there, the fear on her face made me cry harder. She hugged me and asked what the doctors had said. I explained that they were giving me intravenous fluids because I was dehydrated but that they couldn't tell me anything until I had a sonogram.

"I can't lose this baby. I can't."

"Dana, don't think that. I'm sure everything is fine."

A doctor wheeled in a machine and I held my breath when the image appeared on the screen. The pregnancy was definitely not ectopic and the fetus's heartbeat was normal, the doctor said. He couldn't explain the pain but said the dehydration might have contributed to it. Miriam and I hugged and sighed heavily.

It was past 1 a.m. when I got home, and Charles had left several messages on my answering machine. I knew I would lie to him in the morning and say that I had turned off the ringer to get some sleep. I would not say how much that day had scared me or how alone I felt. His shoulders were plenty broad, but Charles already had a hundred men leaning on them, and I was determined not to further weigh him down.

I would soon keep another, more difficult secret. It had to do with the tests that screen for fetal abnormalities.

I have always believed that a woman has a right to decide whether to end a pregnancy, but I could not envision choosing to have an abortion myself, even to save my own life. My conviction was based on my faith, unconventional though it was. The God I worshiped understood my quirks and failings and allowed me to be human. He knew that I was trying to live a virtuous life, if not a perfect one. My commitment to my unborn child was part of that faith, and I knew I could never discard my baby because a test determined that he or she was not perfect.

"How would you feel if, God forbid, we had a disabled baby?" I asked Charles one day.

He did not have to think long.

"I'm already praying that we have a healthy baby, but I'll love it no matter what," he said.

"I'm glad you feel that way because I don't want to have any of the prenatal tests doctors tell older mothers they're supposed to have. Is that all right with you?"

Charles said it was. He also believed in my right to make my own decisions about my body.

The next part I did not tell him about.

Early in the second trimester, my doctor recommended that I consult with a genetic counselor and schedule an amniocentesis. When I declined, she was first perplexed, then irritated. She urged me several times to reconsider, then asked if she could order a non-invasive blood test that would screen for Down syndrome but would not provide a definitive diagnosis. I relented simply to satisfy her and move on. The test results were normal, and that seemed the end of the matter. Then, during my next appointment, she sent me for what I assumed was more routine blood work. I was sitting at my desk at work when she called with the results.

One of the tests had revealed a problem, she said: a high risk of Down syndrome.

My heart sank. "What are you talking about? What test?"

She said that she had ordered a more accurate test during my last appointment and the results were different from the previous one. "You need to see a genetic counselor immediately, and I want you to have an amniocentesis quickly."

What she meant was that time was ticking away for me to have an abortion if there was a fetal abnormality. I was furious.

"Ms. Canedy, you're an intelligent woman and I don't understand why you don't want to have all the information available to you," she said. "You don't have to act on it, but if the baby has Down syndrome, it will need specialists and you'll need to prepare yourself."

I hesitated, searching for the right words.

"I'm going on faith that God will give me whatever baby he wants me to have. That doesn't necessarily mean it will be perfectly healthy, but I'll love it regardless," I said. "And if my baby needs specialists, then he or she will have them. This is exactly the path that I didn't want to be on and now you've sent me down it anyway."

I hung up trembling and set about finding a new physician. When I told Charles a week later that I had switched doctors, he wanted to know why. It had to do with my health insurance, I said.

One of my guiding principles is always to look people in the eye and speak the truth. Even so, telling your father those lies seemed like the loving thing to do. His training might determine his survival, and I was concerned that he might lose his concentration if he was anxious about my pregnancy.

As I later found out, Charles was keeping secrets of his own. He had alluded to problems at work but refused to be specific. He also did not tell me until weeks after the fact that he had had laser eye surgery to correct his vision so as to avoid having to wear glasses in the heat in Iraq.

"Why didn't you say something?" I asked, exasperated. "I would have come to take care of you."

"Dana, you didn't need to be flying here pregnant to look after me. I was fine, and it's over with now."

I was upset even though I had no right to be. What else was he not saying?

By the time summer faded into fall, I had a definite baby bulge, and the nausea and fatigue had passed. Charles found time late that October to take a break in his training, and I scheduled an ultrasound appointment for the week of his visit. It would be the first time he would see what I looked like carrying his child.

When he walked into the apartment and saw me standing in front of him, he stared as if I were a rare and fragile flower that he longed to stroke but was too afraid to touch. I laughed and grabbed his hands and placed them on my stomach. He fell to his knees, kissed the spot just below my navel, and rested his head there.

"You look beautiful, Ma," he said when he rose to look into my eyes.

Looking at the sonogram together was magical. I had been attending all my doctor appointments alone until that week and had tried to suppress my sadness at seeing so many other men accompanying their pregnant wives and partners. Now at last my man was beside me.

The technician called us into an exam room, and I hoisted myself up onto the table and lifted my shirt so she could smear cold conduction gel on my stomach. She pulled a chair next to me for Charles and proceeded to maneuver a wand over my belly. Then, there it was, a head and a spine and tiny little fingers. I heard Charles gasp and then he rose to lean over me. He kissed me with such love in his eyes. Then he sat back down, mesmerized, as the technician pointed to a tiny heart and two little feet. She moved the wand around again, and the little life on the screen began to perform, gulping amniotic fluid and raising a hand near an ear.

It was important to us to find out before your father left for Iraq if we were having a boy or a girl. Now, to our joy, we learned that we were expecting a son.

> *I have always wanted a son. You are my miracle child*
> *because I thought it was too late to have more*
> *children. Your mother changed my mind and helped*
> *me to believe it was possible.*

We continued to look at the screen, stunned by our good fortune, captivated.

Then the technician said, "Uh oh."

"Is something wrong?" I asked.

She and Charles laughed.

"Not at all, but boys will be boys."

"What does that mean?"

"He found his privates," Charles said.

"No way!" I said, sitting up to get a better look at the screen. "Are you sure?"

They were laughing at me now.

"Oh honey, he's just discovering his body," the technician said.

"Well, don't take a picture of that," I said.

We packed all we could into that precious week, spending hours looking at cribs. I decided on a black wooden model with sleek lines and a mattress with memory foam for added support.

"Memory foam?" Charles said, furrowing his brow. "What does a baby need with a memory foam mattress?"

I was crestfallen.

"Charles, we have to support his little head and back," I said. It was as if he had asked why we needed diapers.

"I might have to get another job to pay for it, but if this is the one you want, we'll get it," he said.

I turned my attention to a CD player that could be attached to the side of the crib. "We'll need it to play lullabies," I said before he could register an objection.

I made a mental note to come back another time for the wet-wipes warmer.

It was too soon to be buying car seats and changing tables, but we did anyway, because I wanted your father to participate in as much of my pregnancy as possible—to carry with him the memory of shopping for his "miracle child." That week it was as though Charles was trying to memorize everything about me. He watched me walk, stomach poking out; followed me into the kitchen when I cooked; and gazed at my image in the bathroom mirror as I applied my makeup.

As I lay in his arms one night, I felt a gentle thumping and grabbed his hand. "Feel this," I said, placing his hand on my belly. He could not detect the movement.

"Soon," I said. "You'll be able to feel it soon."

I wanted so desperately for him to feel the little kicks before he left.

After that visit, he became even more protective, which made me grateful but at times tested my patience. We were both on edge as the day of his departure for Iraq drew closer.

"What are you doing, Ma?" he asked on the phone one evening.

"Making a cup of tea," I said.

"Well, don't reach over your head in the cabinet to get the cup," he said.

"Excuse me?"

"My mom said that if you reach over your head when you're pregnant the umbilical cord can get wrapped around the baby's neck and strangle it."

"Charles, that's just an old wives' tale," I said.

"Well, my mom's a nurse and she said it's true," he insisted.

"I'm telling you, it's not true and, besides, your mother didn't work in labor and delivery."

"Don't talk about my mother," he snapped.

"What? I'm not talking about your mother. I'm just saying that I'm not going to kill this baby by making tea. What *will* hurt the baby, though, is stress, and you're stressing me out. I'm done with this conversation."

"Well I'm not talking to you, either," he shot back.

We hung up in a huff.

When I answered the phone the next morning, the first thing I heard was Charles laughing, and I joined him.

"What was *that*?" Charles asked.

"Prenatal anxiety, I guess."

"This baby must be thinking, 'God, you gave me crazy parents,'" he said.

Although we had spent hours choosing baby paraphernalia, we had put off deciding when to get married.

"We could go on a weekend cruise before you leave and get married there," I said.

I knew from his silence that he was not emotionally prepared to board a party ship while getting ready for a war, not even to marry me. I wondered, too, whether I wanted to rush the wedding because I feared he might die before I became his wife.

I finally asked, "Do you think we should wait until you come home to get married? It feels like we're trying to cram a lifetime into a few months."

Ever chivalrous, he said he wanted whatever I wanted. I knew he did not want me to think that he had had a change of heart. So I made the call; we would wait. With only six weeks until his deployment, we had no time and energy to plan a wedding anyway. We gambled on having a lifetime to make our family official.

Even with that faith, though, it was time to put Charles's affairs in order.

On a cold gray afternoon in early November, fitting weather for the bleak business before us, we sat at the dining room table going through a stack of documents. He had made out a stack of checks so that I could withdraw money from his account each month. He had also obtained a power of attorney that permitted me to sign on his behalf for military dependent benefits. He told me precisely when his combat pay would be deposited and how much he expected to save while he was away toward a down payment on a bigger apartment in New York and his daughter Christina's college education.

"I won't need to spend much money over there, so it'll really add up," he said proudly.

Then he handed me another document. "Put this someplace safe," he said, "in case you need it." I looked down and saw my name. It was a copy of the form designating his life insurance beneficiaries.

I wanted the conversation to be over, but there was more to discuss.

"Charles," I said, my voice cracking, "If, God forbid, you should die over there, where do you want to be buried?"

He seemed at a loss. I asked if he would prefer his hometown or Arlington National Cemetery.

"Arlington would be good. It would be easier for everybody to come visit me."

I felt a catch in my throat and stood up and walked to the bay window in the living room. Then I turned back to him. "Sweetheart, would you want me to plan your funeral?" I managed to ask.

"Absolutely not," Charles said. "If something happens to me, you just take care of my son."

I felt the tears welling up.

"Would you worry about my ability to raise him alone?"

"No," he said. "Dana, I trust you more than anyone in my life. You're going to be a great mother."

"Can I ask you something else?" He looked at me as if I were asking for permission to breathe.

"Woman, when have I ever been able to stop you from interviewing me?"

"I'm not interviewing you. I'm just curious about something."

"What do you want to know?"

"When people go away to war, what do they do about sex?"

Charles had gotten used to my bizarre questions, but this one was strange even for me. He looked puzzled for a second but then realized I was serious and tried to give me a thoughtful answer.

"Well, when you first get over there, you're so scared that sex is the furthest thing from your mind. You're just thinking about surviving and getting used to the conditions and the sounds. After a while, some soldiers do have affairs. I'm not going to lie."

"With who?" I asked.

"Why do you want to know?"

"I was just thinking that if you need sex in Iraq, I mean to help get you through whatever you're going to be facing, I want you to know that you have my permission."

He looked at me as though I must be having some sort of pre-postpartum delusion.

"Have you lost your mind?"

"No, I'm completely serious. I can't even imagine what being in a war is like. So I don't know how you cope in that environment.

If you get over there and you find you need somebody to hold, to get through it, I don't want you to feel guilty. There's nothing you could do in combat that I would hold against you. Just make sure you protect yourself at all times."

Charles was flabbergasted.

I was making lunch a short time later and he came in the kitchen. He slid his arms around me and palmed my belly. "You are carrying my child," he said. "I would never disrespect you by doing anything like that, you crazy woman."

With all this talk of war and death gratuities and final wishes, the time seemed right to give Charles a gift I had been saving for him—something that had caught my eye at a stationery store.

It was a journal.

Not a blank book—a "guided" journal for fathers, with a question at the top of each page. The first one I spotted asked the writer to describe his childhood. Perhaps this would encourage Charles to jot down a few thoughts for the son he had not yet met.

He sat silently on our bed, thumbing through the pages. Nearly an hour later, I found him sitting in that same spot, already writing. He wrote well into the night and for much of the next morning. He took it into the bathroom with him, wrote while he ate, and brought it to bed.

How do you treat a woman? Jordan, I think if you have read this far you should certainly know how to treat a woman. Treat every woman with respect. If you take her out on a date, treat her like a queen. You may never go out with her again but I guarantee you will leave a lasting impression.

> *Never hit a woman because a man who hits a*
> *woman is not a true man. Always keep a mutual*
> *platform, meaning respect is mutual. . . . Women are*
> *extraordinary people. Learn all you can from them.*

As Charles's deployment drew frighteningly near, I began to accept the fact of his leaving. When I was five months pregnant, he made a final trip to New York for Thanksgiving and I took a week off from work. I was determined to remain upbeat, but inevitably something would upset me—like the way he kept twisting his arm and wincing. He said it was sore from the many vaccinations he had been required to get. He had received all but the one against anthrax, which wasn't recommended for anyone who might come in contact with a pregnant woman.

"Don't you need it?" I asked, alarmed.

"I'm not going to take anything that might hurt you or the baby."

For the rest of the evening I worried about whether he would survive an anthrax attack. I was afraid to find out what else he had been vaccinated against, and Charles was determined to change the subject. He succeeded in distracting me when he said that there was a special item he wanted to buy the next day.

The following afternoon your father and I stood just inside the entrance of a baby superstore, feeling as lost as if we were at NASA headquarters. There were vast floors of baby gear that I wondered how my mother ever did without: a teddy bear that made simulated womb sounds, a talking potty, vibrating bouncy seats.

Our first stop was for Charles's special item: an outfit for a newborn. He wanted me to have one that he had chosen in case I went into labor and delivered early and he missed your birth. If all went according to plan, however, Charles would be with me. He would take his allotted two-week leave early, and the doctor would induce my labor a week before my due date to help us coordinate our schedules.

I beamed as Charles searched the clothing racks and touched fabrics, trying to choose the softest one. Eventually he settled on a blue fleece sweat suit with a hood and an emblem of a football on the jacket. It looked too big for a newborn, but when he held it up and smiled, I knew it was an image I would hold on to for the rest of my life.

"It just killed you to let me pick it by myself, didn't it?" Charles said, laughing.

I assured him that I wouldn't have wanted it any other way. "I can't wait for us to show it to our son one day and tell him that his daddy bought it for him to wear home from the hospital," I said. "Maybe he'll put it on his own son someday."

I had never seen a man happier than your father was at that moment. But then I thought of what was coming. I said that I could not stand the thought of him spending Christmas alone and in danger. He said I had already given him the most precious gift of all.

> *I think the best Christmas gift is knowing that I will have a son soon. Trust me, I love your sister, but having a son will be an added surprise to my life. While I sit here in Iraq, I feel blessed to know that you are coming to a great family.*

My belly felt heavy and my back ached, but I was determined to cook what I knew would be our last holiday meal together until he returned from the war.

> *The Thanksgiving I spent with your mother before I left for Iraq will always be the most memorable. Your mother was pregnant with you. I tried to talk her out of cooking but she insisted. It was a great week. We spent three full days shopping for you, spending time together, and getting much needed rest.*
>
> *Dinner was great. Your mom cooked Cornish hen, dressing, cranberry salad, mashed potatoes with green beans. It was one of the best times we spent together. I'm thankful for that.*

I was walking past Charles in our bedroom that Thanksgiving Day when I thought about what our lives would be like the same time the next year.

"Just think, we will have even more to be thankful for next Thanksgiving," I said. "You'll be home for good and our baby boy will be here with us."

Charles did not say a word—he just handed me a large framed drawing. It was one of his angel pictures. He had drawn a series of them the previous year and had donated them to a benefit for cancer survivors. This one depicted a man's chiseled body with an enormous, stunning pair of angel wings attached to his back. The man was bowed in prayer and was clearly presenting himself to God.

"I don't want this," I said, shoving the picture back at Charles.

"Take this back. This is a picture of *you*. Don't give me a picture of you as an angel. You're coming home."

Charles thought I would take comfort from the image, but I was shaking so badly I had to sit down. I had been trying to pretend, for just one day, that we were an average couple celebrating an ordinary Thanksgiving, but the angel snapped me out of the dream.

He said nothing and put the picture in a closet. I later learned that just before he left for Iraq he gave his mother and several close friends the same drawing.

Later, he sat by a window writing in the journal and occasionally lifted his pen, contemplative, before he continued. He had replaced many of the questions at the top of each page with ones he had written himself. One said: "What was your most painful experience during Desert Storm?" He wrote:

I was a young sergeant during Desert Storm. I was the platoon sergeant's gunner. We had a crazy tank commander in our platoon. His name was SSG. Summerall. He always had good advice about setting goals for yourself. He always told me not to worry about what other people have to say. Do what you think is right. Somehow he knew my frustration because I was a quiet soldier.

One day our platoon had guard duty. SSG. Summerall stepped on an explosive bomblet. The medics did all they could for him. We had to continue guard mission when the commander told us that night

*that he had passed away. That was hard, continuing
to work with a fallen soldier in the platoon. God
bless him.*

I am glad not to have read entries like that one before Charles
left. It would have made it that much harder for me to say good-bye
to him.

I told him that he didn't need to exhaust himself, that he could
take the journal with him.

"No," he said, "I have to finish this before I leave."

One morning I walked into the bathroom and saw him sitting
on the toilet with the lid down, writing while the shower was going.
"Sweetie, you really don't have to do this," I said. He stopped and
considered.

"Maybe I'll take it with me," he said, set the journal down, and
got in the shower. I knew then that he was mentally prepared to
leave for Iraq.

The evening before he returned to Fort Hood, I took him to a
steak house and told him to order the biggest steak on the menu.
We held hands and talked about how nice the crib would look in
our room. Charles made me promise to be careful walking on the
snow and ice that winter and pleaded with me not to take on too
many projects at work. He assured me that he would come home
when I gave birth. I rubbed his arm and said I would be fine until
he returned. I reminded him that my pregnancy was going well and
that I was surrounded by friends and caring colleagues.

It was a chilly evening, but we took our time walking, oblivious
to the other people hurrying past. It would be our last evening
together for a very long while, and both of us wanted the night to

unfold as slowly as possible. We had decided to see a movie as our last date before we became new parents, and sat through a bad romantic comedy about a bachelor trying to win the affections of his high school crush. The ridiculous dialogue would ordinarily have annoyed me, but it was good to hear Charles laugh. I rested my head on his shoulder and we kissed between scenes.

All too soon the darkness gave way to dawn. We untangled ourselves and knew it was time to face the difficult morning ahead. I wrote a letter to Charles while he was in the shower and tucked it into his bag. He discovered the envelope while packing the last of his things and I asked him not to open it until he was on the plane to Iraq.

The doorman rang to tell us that the car I had ordered to take Charles to the airport had arrived. Then I broke down.

Charles kissed my swollen stomach as I stood shaking and sobbing by the front door. He placed the palms of his hands on my belly and sighed in his own anguish. I pressed his head into me. Both of us held on as long as we could. Then he stood up, wiped away my tears, and said softly that he loved me. I could see in his face that a whisper was all he could speak. And then he left.

I did not want him to hear me sobbing again, so I waited until I was sure he was on the elevator, then cried until my head ached and my eyes stung. I went back to bed and cried myself to sleep.

Charles called from Texas several hours later as he was driving from the airport to the base. I could tell that his focus had already begun to change. He talked about shipping his art to me and where he would store his truck. He would need to disconnect his cell phone and go to the pharmacy to stock up on eyedrops. And there was the issue of where he would sleep in the days ahead. He had moved out of his apartment and put his furniture in storage the day before he flew to New York, but he still had a week until deployment. I told him to check into the nicest hotel he could find, order room service, and watch pay-per-view movies. He told me he had a cot in his office and would sleep there.

"Charles, you are *not* sleeping in your office on your last days in this country. You deserve to treat yourself well. Check into a hotel. I'll pay for it."

"I don't need to stay in a hotel," he said.

"But where are you going to take a shower?" I asked.

"At the barracks," he said.

"Charles, please. Why?"

He hesitated.

"I don't want to spend money on a hotel. We need to save it for the baby."

Every night that week he called from his office, and each time I pleaded with him to go to a hotel. One of his soldiers, Kenny Morris, and his wife, Donna, had offered him a spare room in their house, but Donna said she suspected he wanted to give her family privacy during their last days together.

By the end of that week, I had come to realize that forgoing the comfort of a bed was not just about saving money. It was part of his mental transformation from the man I knew into the warrior I did not. The instant he walked out my door, he was no longer just my man and the father of my child. He was a soldier headed for war.

The night before he left, Charles settled into that cot and called me one last time. He told me not to worry about him, to take care of myself. He told me he would contact me as soon as he could after getting there. I told him that I was proud of him and would try to be strong.

"Charles, can I ask you something?" I said.

"Sure, Ma, what?"

"Can you think of anything we haven't talked about? Anything left unsaid?"

He thought for a minute and said he could not.

"Well then, if you have to go, I'm so thankful that we can't think of a single thing that we haven't said to each other. Isn't that a blessing?"

"Yes, it is," he said.

"I love you, Charles."

"I love you, too, Dana."

He said he had my letter in his carry-on bag and would read it as soon as he was in the air. He said that he knew it would sustain him during the journey ahead. No words I had ever written were more important than these:

Charles, my love,

Thank you for the gift of your heart. I do not feel worthy of your love, but I cherish it and thank God every day that he led me to you.

I am so in awe of you, my brave man, and I am so proud that you are the father of my baby.

When you have fulfilled your duty, please come safely home to us. I cannot wait to spend the rest of my life as your wife.

Do not worry about us: focus on protecting yourself and I will take care of myself and your son.

With all that I am, I love you,
Dana

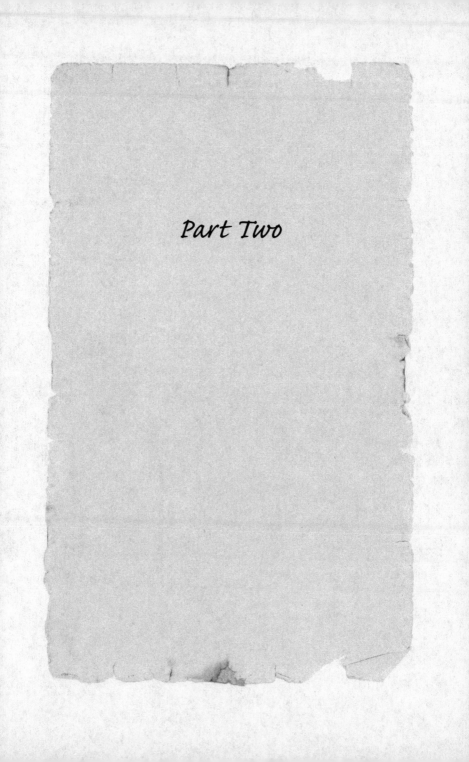

Part Two

Nine

Dear Jordan,

In the months before I gave birth to you, I had two hearts beating inside of me, and from the moment my Charles left for the war, one of them was broken.

He left his scent in our bed and a note on my pillow, inside a card made from his angel print.

To my Sunshine, Dana,

I knew that it would be difficult to say good-bye. Yes, I am praying that I will be able to return and help you with Jordan. He will be such a blessing to you and everyone that meets him. I think he is going to be so special. Thank you, God, for our little miracle.

I must write this so you can read it from time to time. Thank you for everything you have taught me. Thank you for the great times we have had together. Thank you for being my best friend, a friend who has always been honest, loving, and caring. Most of all, thank you for Jordan, our son.

Thank you for being a counselor and standing by me when I needed it. Thank you for reaching out to me and showing me that you loved me for who I am.

I ask you to forgive me for any pain I have caused you. I love you very much. I will miss you and think about you and Jordan.

Love, Charles

The words were soothing, but even in that joyous time—with the weight of your growing body inside me, and the occasional jab of a foot in my ribs—they were not enough to dispel the worrying.

The first weeks without him were the hardest. I did not have a phone number for Charles and he was only able to check his e-mail sporadically. I immersed myself in work and took comfort in the knowledge that in early December of 2005 your father was likely still training in Kuwait and had not yet crossed the border into more treacherous territory. Still, if the phone rang after dark, I jumped, fearing the unthinkable. I had told Charles that if something awful happened, I did not want to be called at work or on my cell phone, only at home. He kissed the corner of my mouth and explained that, if the worst happened, military representatives would visit rather than call. He would ask his family to call me only at home with bad news.

As the weeks without him wore on, it was increasingly hard to stay composed. Television sets throughout the newsroom were continually tuned to news programs, and because of my responsibility for breaking national coverage, one of them sat squarely on my desk. Often a large "Breaking News" banner would appear on the screen, and I would instinctively turn to it. The report might be about a courtroom shooting in Atlanta or a school bus crash in Fort Lauderdale—events that I would need to assign a reporter to cover. Or it might be about something far more personal: more dead American soldiers in Iraq.

"Don't watch that," one of my colleagues would call from behind a nearby desk. If the coverage was particularly grim, someone would turn the television away from my view or shut it off.

Other reminders were harder to screen out. An editor who sat across from me was in charge of tracking American casualties in Iraq. Whenever the military released new numbers, she would shout, without looking up from her computer, to a clerk who kept the tally, "I've got more dead guys!" No one seemed to flinch but me. I never got up the courage to ask her to handle it differently; I feared I would break down if I had to put into words the way her broadcasts tore through me.

The one thing that could distract me was a challenging story, so I kept up the ten-hour workdays throughout the winter, by which time my belly bulged so much that people on the subway gave up their seats for me each morning. My due date was March 25, and by the middle of January my colleagues began to ask when I was planning to ease up.

"Still here?" someone would ask when I walked into the office every morning. An editor started an office pool on when I would give birth—it grew to two hundred dollars. One colleague offered to split the winnings with me if I would arrange to give birth on the date he had selected. To the woman who chose the day that was furthest away, I said, "I hope you lose. I want this baby out soon."

My girlfriends flew in from all over the country and hosted a baby shower in a private room at a gourmet restaurant. My colleagues had another shower in the grand, glass-enclosed executive reception room that looks out onto Times Square. My boss took up a collection for a stroller. The editor who tracked casualties gave me a yellow and blue sweater with duck-shaped buttons that she had knitted. A feisty reporter whom I never would have imagined in a kitchen baked cookies in the shape of baby rattles. The publisher hugged me and joked about my "making deadline" for the biggest assignment of my life.

Of course, with journalists as hosts, I was showered not only with gifts but with questions. Had I started to dilate yet? Was I planning to have an epidural?

I ignored the question about my cervix but announced, "They can hook me up with the drugs now."

Someone asked whether Charles would be able to make it back in time for the birth. "Yes, thank goodness. I couldn't imagine going through this without him," I said. "Besides, meeting his son will help keep his morale up until he comes home for good."

Most days, that thought buoyed my spirits, even during the long periods of silence between Charles's phone calls. The day the crib arrived was not one of them. As the deliverymen put it together, I had to push out of my head the vision of your father assembling it himself. Of course, if he had, we surely would have fought over which rail was supposed to be attached to what spring. He would have huffed at me to let him figure it out. I would have crossed my arms and watched him struggle until I could no longer resist pointing out that he was doing it all wrong.

It was an argument I wished we could have.

While the men finished with the crib, I distracted myself by writing Charles a letter—enclosing pictures of my naked belly, taken as a shower gift by my gay friend Ciro. Charles and I wrote often, but it had been weeks since we had talked. I longed to hear his voice and let him know that I could almost make out an elbow and a foot when I felt those increasingly sharp kicks.

He finally called in early February while I was lying in bed reading, and I placed the phone on my stomach so he could talk to you.

"He's kicking," I said when I put the receiver back to my ear. "I think he can hear you."

I tried to imagine pride on Charles's face, but there was only weariness in his voice.

"How are you feeling, Ma?" he asked.

I told him I was all right, just worried about him. He said he was fine, too, but "definitely gainfully employed." He told me not to worry, that I had enough on my mind already.

The conversation was innocuous, but something about it made me uneasy. He would not elaborate on where he had been and what he had been doing. He had warned me in a letter that the military monitored our calls and to be careful what I said. I was incensed at that. Was it really necessary for someone to listen in while we discussed the pros and cons of circumcision?

Later, reading the journal, I would question whether he had ever been "fine" in Iraq. But even if Charles had been able to speak freely in our phone calls, he would have said little about his missions for fear of upsetting me during the final stage of my pregnancy. He seemed to want to talk about anything but himself.

"You look beautiful, Ma," he told me one Saturday evening, after he had received the pictures. "I love the belly."

"That's because you're not the one who has to carry this baby around!" I said. "I can't wait until he gets here. I'm ready to meet him. Thank God the crib arrived in time."

He asked how the crib looked in the room. I told him about the light blue sheets and quilt and the teddy bear mobile hanging above it. I told him that a friend had given us six months' worth of diapers and that we had two strollers. I told him that you had more clothes than the two of us combined.

"Wait until you see all this stuff," I said. "Which reminds me, you need to let me know soon when you're coming so I can set a date to be induced."

"Uh, I don't know, Ma," Charles said.

"You must have *some* idea. Haven't you put in the request for your leave?"

"No," he said.

"Well, what are you waiting for? You're cutting it kind of close."

"I don't know, Ma."

"You don't know what?"

He said nothing.

"Charles?"

"What?"

"What are you telling me?"

More silence.

"You're not coming home, are you?" I said.

"Ma, please try to understand. I just got my guys settled and I have to be here for them. They need me. I'm sorry, but I'm going to be the last one to go home."

He had made his decision and nothing I said was going to change it—but I pleaded with him nonetheless.

"Who's going to hold my hand? I can't do this without you," I said.

I began to sob. I knew he was less than three months into his tour of duty, but I had never considered that the warrior's priorities would win out over the father's. He had promised to be there beside me.

"Dana, I don't think you understand a first sergeant's job. I'm responsible for a whole company of men and most of them are real young. They're just adjusting to being in combat. I couldn't forgive myself if one of them got injured or killed while I was gone."

My pain turned to anger. I gripped the phone tighter, my hands shaking. It was hard to breathe. I had to stand up, to pace. I said, "Those men could get hurt or killed whether you're there or not. And it's not like I'm asking you to go on a cruise. *We* are your family—this baby and me. We need you as much as they do. I want us to be together when we meet our son. I want to see both of your faces when he's born. Please don't do this."

"I'm sorry, Dana, but I can't come," he said. "Please try to understand."

I told him I didn't understand and he sighed deeply, clearly in his own agony.

I wanted to tell him that I would never forgive him. I wanted to say that all the love I had ever felt for him had just drained out of me. I wanted to say that it was over between us, that I did not ever want to hear from him again. I wanted to tell him to go to hell.

But what if those were the last words he ever heard me speak?

I could not risk it. I simply said I was tired and needed to take a nap.

"All right, I'll call you later," he said feebly and hung up.

I threw a framed picture of him against the wall, shattering the glass. Then I gathered up all the other pictures of him and shoved them into a dresser drawer. I paced, crying, before falling to my knees, rocking and hugging my belly. I hated him.

Between frequent trips to the bathroom and my disbelief over Charles's decision, I did not get much rest that night. I finally fell asleep sometime before dawn and awoke late Sunday morning to feel you squirming inside me.

"Someone is hungry," I said, patting my belly.

I turned on some music and fixed a cup of tea and some toast with strawberry preserves. Then I phoned Miriam, who bore the emotional weight of my pregnancy more and more. After our trip to the emergency room, she had agreed to attend a childbirth class with me and be my labor coach in case Charles did not make it home in time. She was a calm spirit, just what I would need when the pain of labor hit. She told me she would be honored and was excited by the prospect of seeing a baby born.

Within a week, two other women I loved had signed on to be there for the big day. My mother would fly to New York two weeks before my due date and stay until after I came home from the hospital. My friend Katti, a writer and one of the sassiest free spirits I had ever encountered, wanted to be there, too.

"Trust me, women are a lot more helpful during labor than men anyway," my doctor said when I told her that I would not need to be induced after all. She placed a hand on my shoulder and said that it would be "just us girls" when I delivered. Once I finally accepted that Charles was not going to be a part of the birth, I began to relax and warm to the idea of celebrating your new life in the company of three women I knew would love and protect you from the moment you arrived.

Even so, I could not help feeling sorry for myself when Miriam and I walked into the first childbirth class and everyone seemed to stare. As I waddled to the back of the room to grab one of the dolls the instructor told us to take, I told myself that I would not have minded if they thought we were lesbians. What I absolutely did not want them to think was that I was just another pregnant black woman without a man. As I perched on a metal chair and listened as the instructor welcomed us, I felt a need to make sure that no one thought I had gotten knocked up by some no-good man who could not even be bothered to attend a childbirth class. So when it came time to introduce ourselves, I said that my name was Dana and that my friend Miriam was graciously standing in for the father of my baby, who was a soldier fighting in Iraq.

Suddenly I was the star of the class. Several of the husbands offered to help me up from the floor after the breathing exercises. One mother-to-be said she admired my strength. But instead of being relieved, I felt foolish. I knew that in a couple of weeks I would never see these people again, so why had I made such a point of telling them my business? While I was feeling defensive, they were probably focused on their own prenatal anxieties. But I could not help it: I wanted them to know that the father of my child deserved their respect. He had not abandoned me. He was protecting each one of them. He was missing his baby's birth for them. He was putting his life on the line for *them*. And I was living through it with him.

Meanwhile, Charles tried to help me understand that he had not made the decision lightly. In deciding to have a baby with me at a time when he knew he would miss most of my pregnancy and the initial period of bonding with you, he had postponed his own happiness. He did so because he did not want to leave this earth without making me the mother of his child. For that, I owed him my loyalty and continued love. Each day I forgave him a little more.

A fierce snowstorm blew in that Valentine's Day. I was lounging in the living room listening to music when the doorman rang to say that there was a delivery—a gorgeous vase of roses, lilies, daisies, and other flowers. A teddy bear was hugging the vase, and balloons floated above it.

I ripped open the card.

"Happy Valentine's Day, Ma," it said. "Love, Charles."

I was stunned. I announced to the poor deliveryman that if my fiancé could order flowers from Iraq, then no other man on the planet had an excuse not to remember his wife or girlfriend on Valentine's Day. I felt like the queen Charles had always said I was.

By the end of February, Charles did his best to call me every other day, but we had also enlisted a network of military wives to get the word to him when I went into labor. Not once did I worry that they would not be able to find him. They are a unique brand of brave, the military spouses who keep small businesses going and homework checked and cars tuned up while their husbands—or wives—are away. I was ashamed that I had ever resisted becoming one of them.

"Babe, you let me know when the time comes and we'll find him," said Donna Morris, whose husband, Sergeant First Class Kenneth R. Morris, was one of Charles's soldiers and a friend. The plan was that as soon as I let her know that I was in labor, Donna would call and send e-mails to the wives in Charles's company. If one of them received a phone call from her husband that day, she would tell him to "find the First Sergeant." The wives would also send urgent e-mails to their men with the same instructions.

The evening of March 27, that is just what happened.

My mother and I had been playing Scrabble much of that day and I was ahead by about 100 points in our latest round when I could no longer ignore the intensifying pain in my belly.

"I think I ought to call my doctor," I said.

My mother is about as calm as a hurricane, and she was thunderstruck when I told her I needed to take a shower and do my hair and makeup before following my doctor's orders to go to the hospital.

"I can't meet my baby looking like this! It will be his first image of his mommy and I don't want to scare him."

The contractions seemed to ease when the warm water hit my stomach but they began again when I started applying plum eye shadow and black mascara. I gripped the sink and stared into the bathroom mirror. Someone clearly had mistaken my stomach for a wet towel and was wringing it out. I felt the urge to vomit. My mother had a look of sheer terror on her face. Miriam had arrived and was behind her, instructing me to breathe.

"Stop that!" I said, "I tried it and it doesn't work. I want my money back from those birth class people."

The cab to the hospital was the only one in New York City with a driver who could not find Broadway, Manhattan's most prominent thoroughfare. "Are you kidding me?" I yelled as he made a wrong turn while I was in the middle of a contraction. When my mother noticed his accent and asked about his home country, I interjected, "Who cares? He needs to concentrate on where he's going, not where he came from."

Miriam gently tried to urge more "*hee hee*" breathing exercises to calm me down.

"I said I'm not doing that," I snapped.

Maybe Charles was lucky not to have been there. My mean Gemini twin had taken over.

When the cab finally pulled into Columbia Presbyterian, the nice Dana returned and apologized to the driver—but probably only because I was between contractions.

The good vibe did not last when the gum-chewing receptionist with psychedelic nails chose not to break off her personal phone call, and when the resident cheerfully suggested I walk to the delivery area to speed up my labor. I have always had a low tolerance for pain and choose dentists primarily by how liberally they use nitrous oxide. I had never intended to be one of those people who embrace natural childbirth as some essential rite of womanhood. As far as I was concerned, there was nothing natural about feeling as if someone was playing tug-o-war with my insides. So I began pleading for an epidural almost as soon as we arrived.

Once I was settled into the birthing room, Miriam briefly let go of my hand to grab my "focal point," a calming object from birth class that was supposed to help us center ourselves during contractions. Mine was an adorable school photograph of my nephew

Cameron who was beaming at me as I focused on the ball tightening up in my belly.

Maybe those childbirth people were not all phonies, I thought, as I smiled at Cameron. The feeling did not last, and I began once again to beg for an epidural.

As my mother stroked me, I could have read her mind. She wanted to bolt for a cigarette. I have to give her credit; she held off.

Miriam had returned from trying to find my nurse when the angel of epidurals walked into the room pushing a cart of needles and tubes. He started going over a consent form but I wanted my drugs. I grabbed it from him and said, "Fine, if you paralyze me I'll forgive you. Just show me where to sign." I scribbled a name that looked vaguely like mine and promptly threw up.

Then, finally, the epidural: a pinch, a bit of pressure, and then sheer pleasure. Not even Charles had ever made me feel that good. I heard myself laughing when the doctor said I had a skinny spine. At that moment, it was the most hilarious thing I had ever heard. Miriam and my mom returned just as my good twin reemerged. Hugs all around, and then we slept.

Soon, though, I was woken by an insistent beeping. My upbeat nurse had turned solemn and was staring at a screen. She pulled a phone out of her pocket and punched a button. Almost immediately, the epidural angel emerged and stuck a needle into my IV.

"What's going on?" I asked.

"The baby's heartbeat dropped," the nurse said. "But we have it under control."

At 5 a.m. there was a tap on my arm and my doctor was there, explaining that your heartbeat was irregular and that they had given me a drug called Pitocin to try to speed my labor. However, the contractions had stopped, she said. My water had broken but I was still only four centimeters dilated.

"We need to do a C-section," the doctor said.

My mother's cell phone rang and she left the room.

"It was Charles calling from Iraq," she said when she returned. "One of the wives got ahold of her husband and he told him you were in the hospital."

"Mom, why didn't you give me the phone?" I practically yelled.

"You were talking to the doctor. He's going to call back."

A team of doctors and nurses came in to prepare me for surgery and my mom popped out of the room again. They were about to wheel me away when she returned, smelling of cigarette smoke. The thought of my newborn inhaling the scent of cigarettes made me rethink the choice I had made when the doctor said only one person could accompany me into the operating room. I suddenly longed for Charles. I wanted so badly for him to have been the one rushing down the hallway beside my gurney and into an operating room with canary yellow walls and classical musical softly playing. I wanted him to be the one sitting beside me while the doctors were cutting and tugging behind a blue screen that blocked my view from the chest down.

I tried to relax, taking deep breaths of oxygen through the tube in my nostrils, and wondered whether Charles was thinking about us at that very moment. I imagined him pacing in the desert.

The doctor's voice and some vigorous tugging on my midsection got my attention just in time to keep me from feeling sorry for myself.

"Are you ready to meet your baby?" the doctor asked. "Does he have a name?"

"Jordan," I said.

"Hello there, Jordan," she said. "Happy Birthday!"

You had just made our family complete.

I heard a soft cry that reminded me of a chirping baby bird. It was the loveliest sound I have ever heard. Then, over the blue screen, your tiny red face emerged, with squinting eyes and a head full of sandy brown and blond hair. Your long legs were wiggling, tiny fingers moving.

I gasped and began to cry. I heard my mother gasp, too. You were so very beautiful.

I was still strapped to the table but I managed to lift my head just enough to kiss your soft face and lips. I breathed you in, the sweet smell of a miracle.

> *I could not be at your birth because of the war, but you were surrounded by strong women when you were born. All of these women embody the reasons you should never, ever disrespect or lay your hand against a woman. Remember who taught you to speak, to walk, and to be a gentleman. These are your first teachers, my little prince. Protect them, embrace them, and always treat them like a queen. Women with outward beauty are a dime a dozen, but [being with] a woman with these qualities of loyalty, trust, and caring for who you really are will have a lot more meaning. Never listen to your friends—follow your heart and look for the strength of a woman.*

Miriam and Katti were waiting when a nurse wheeled me into the recovery room. While you were suckling I boasted to them that you got a 9.9 on your Apgar test. "And did you see how fast he just latched on? This kid is obviously very advanced."

We finally settled into a private room about an hour later and I

Left: My mother, Penny Canedy, at age seventeen. I was born two years later.

Right: My father, T. J. Canedy, in an undated photograph early in his military career.

Can you believe this is your mom? I was about six.

Your aunt Lynnette and me (left) at about four and five years old, showing off our Afros outside the "quarters" where we lived on Fort Knox army base.

Your dad was handsome even as a boy. Here he is at about age seven.

Your grandpa King and grandma King with your aunt Gail and your father.

Me as a cub reporter in the *Plain Dealer* newsroom in Cleveland.

Though he was a highly decorated soldier, your father rarely spoke of his accolades, except to say that he wanted you to inherit his medals.

Your dad and me getting ready to board a cruise ship. He was already in vacation mode. I had come straight from the office and was carrying an envelope full of work. Your father offered to carry my briefcase, of course.

Your father asked to see pictures of my growing belly while he was in Iraq. This one was taken in a park near our home when I was eight and a half months pregnant.

Your father was headed back to the operating base after searching for three straight days and nights for two missing American soldiers when he stopped to introduce himself to this group of Iraqi children.

In this photograph, which he printed on a color printer and inscribed in Iraq, he is leading his young soldiers to a memorial for one of their fallen comrades.

You were just hours old in this picture, which your godmother Miriam took to send to your dad.

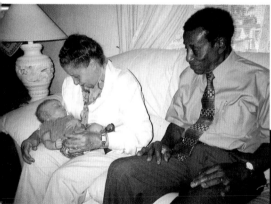

You were a few weeks old in this photograph, and I was one proud new mother.

Here you are with your grandmother and grandfather King the day they met you. You look just like your grandmother, which made your father proud.

Here we are at church, me listening to the sermon and you skipping it.

You and your father about twenty
minutes after you first met.

One week later.

One of our
only family
photos.
It sits on my
nightstand.

You were so solemn at your father's funeral, as if you somehow understood the magnitude of the moment.

Here we are at the cemetery with your sister, Christina, and your grandfather and grandmother King as we bid farewell to your father.

Leaving my Charles's side at the cemetery was excruciating.

Your sister, Christina, flew to New York for your first birthday. She adores you.

This picture was also taken at your first birthday party, which was attended by more than sixty friends and relatives from all over the country. I was determined to make that day a celebration of life, even though our family was still grieving.

Here you are at age two. I wish your father could see what a happy and outgoing child you are.

This extraordinary angel print, which your father drew, hangs above your bed.

took you out of your blanket and marveled at your long arms and spindly legs and, to my utter shock, the most striking blue eyes I had ever seen.

"Blue eyes," I said, "where did you get those, little guy?"

You were the most glorious sight, but you looked nothing like I had thought you would. For months I had pictured you as an apple-butter-brown baby with dark eyes and curly black hair. In reality, your skin was entirely pink, and flecks of blond hair framed your face. I assumed you took your color from Charles's mother and your blue eyes from his uncle, although recessive genes being what they are, my relatives obviously had something to do with your unique, angelic look.

I had asked the doctor who delivered you as well as two nurses and a pediatrician whether you had Down syndrome. Each one assured me that you did not.

"You want to know something, Jordan? Mommy is just forty years old, but as of this moment, I have already had the best day of my life. I sure wish your daddy was here to see you, but I want you to know that he already loves you, too."

I wrapped you back in your blanket and put the little cap back on your head. I worried about germs, but I just could not stop kissing you. Your grandmother came back into the room and handed me her cell phone.

"Hello, Ma," Charles said. "Congratulations." He sounded so far away.

"Oh, Charles, we have the most precious son. He is just perfect."

Your dad wanted to know what you looked like. I said you were long and skinny and pale with blue eyes.

"Blue eyes, really?" he asked.

"I wouldn't believe it myself if I wasn't sitting here staring at him," I said.

"Wow," Charles said. "You know my uncle has blue eyes. Jordan's may change though, and the little biscuit might brown up."

While he was talking, I never stopped looking at you. Our little biscuit.

"I'm proud of you, Ma," he said. "You did good. How are you feeling?"

"I'm exhausted but I'm too excited to sleep. They're giving me good drugs, so I don't really feel anything."

I did not tell him that the doctor had discovered your umbilical cord wrapped around your arm when she reached inside of me to pluck you out. Your dad would have surely blamed me for having reached over my head for that teacup all those months before.

I told your father that I loved him. It was the first time I had said it and meant it since our fight about him missing your birth. That was behind us now. All I had eyes for was the softness of your little toes, your tiny mouth with its giant yawns. Watching you sleep in a small metal and glass hospital cart, surrounded by flowers and cards, I was more at peace than I had ever been.

Then I got a visit from a hospital administrator.

"Ms. Canedy, we have a paternity problem," the woman announced in a disapproving tone of voice as she walked through the doorway. "The father signed and dated this acknowledgment form before the baby was born, which makes it invalid."

"That's a bureaucracy problem," I said, "not a paternity problem. And please don't talk to me in that tone."

The month before, I had gone on a hospital tour and learned that I needed Charles to sign the paternity form in order for his name to appear on your birth certificate, since he would not be attending the birth. I sent it to him in Iraq and he signed and returned it to me in two weeks.

"The dates of the signatures of the two parents must match," the administrator said, implacable.

"Ma'am, he's in the military, serving in Iraq," I explained.

Regardless, she said, because of the error, the father's name would be blank on the birth certificate.

"You have to be joking," I said.

"If you were married, we wouldn't have this problem," she responded. "All I would need is your marriage license."

"Ma'am, my marital status is none of your business," I said. "This is insensitive and offensive. Get me your boss."

I was furious. No one but God had the right to judge us for the decision we had made.

Soon, a supervisor stopped by my room. She did not apologize for the woman's behavior, but she did promise to help. "In the worst case scenario you can add the father's name after he returns," she said.

I wanted to shout that he was not at Disney World; he was at war and might never return.

"I don't want a corrected birth certificate," I said instead. "He should be able to have his name on our son's *original* birth certificate. And I certainly don't want to have to tell him about this while he is in Iraq."

The supervisor took my home phone number and promised to get back to me. She never did.

At least the next crisis made me want to laugh rather than cry.

I was sitting in a chair nursing you—it was my third day in the hospital—when I heard an alarm go off outside our door and people scurrying about at the nurses' station. Then the sound of rushing footsteps got closer, and a nurse and two security guards burst into my room.

"Ma'am, is that your baby?" the nurse demanded to know.

"Yes, why?" I said, startled. Instinctively, I held you tightly to me.

"His alarm is going off. Hand me the baby please."

"What?"

As the nurse grabbed you from my breast, I looked down at the electronic security device attached to your ankle. The security guards were by turns glancing at me and at the floor. They seemed uncomfortable.

"*What* is going on?" I said as the nurse checked your identification bracelet to be sure it matched mine.

Then I felt something wet trickling down my belly and realized what the problem was. I had not thought to cover my other breast when I was feeding you, and several ounces of milk had leaked onto your leg and short-circuited the alarm. I dabbed at my chest while the nurse wiped off your leg. The security guards had the tact to look away.

As the nurse and I headed to the nursery to replace the alarm, she pushing you in a cart and me walking slowly because of my incision, I heard guffawing. The security guards, no doubt on their way to fill out an incident report, were cracking up.

"You mean you set off the alarm with your milk?" Charles said, incredulous, when he called later that day. I had never heard him laugh so hard.

As I prepared to take you home, dressed in the blue sweat suit your father had chosen for your homecoming, I could still hear his laughter. I savored the sound, knowing that where he was, there was probably not much to laugh at.

Ten

Dear Jordan,

A friend once said that to have a baby is to discover a whole new level of what it means to be human. She was right, as I discovered when you were born and suddenly there was a life that meant more to me than my own.

Katti drove my mother and me home with you the day I left the hospital, and it was like being in traffic for the first time. All the cars seemed too close to ours as I hovered over the car seat where you slept. When we finally made it, I fretted over whether I had dressed you too warm or too cold. Then, after I had fed, burped, and bathed you, I panicked when you cried, thinking I must have done something wrong.

Your grandmother did all she could to help me in those first, sleep-deprived weeks, and friends rescued me from my solitude. Still, there was no way to replace what I needed most—your dad. He and I were supposed to feel our way through those joyful yet exhausting days together—he assuring me that, no, you had not died of SIDS just because you were not snoring in your sleep; he running to buy the breast pump I thought I would not need; he getting up for the 4 a.m. feeding because my incision hurt. Although it was not just the caregiving that I craved. I longed for Charles to see what I saw: how you smiled in your sleep (I refused to believe it was gas); how you smelled right after your bath; how your head felt nestled in my neck. Those should have been his moments, too—and yours.

Your father called weekly to check on us that first month, and he always wanted to hear every new detail about his "Biscuit."

> *My Little Biscuit,*
>   *Today your mother sent me more photos of you. They were right. You are a handsome baby with a great little personality already. I'm going to have to get home soon so I can get some of those kisses everyone has been getting. I'll see you soon, Little Biscuit.*

There was a new lightness in Charles's voice, a new harmony in his laughter.

"How's he doing, Ma? Bet you don't even have time to miss me."

"Of course I miss you," I said. "I see you every time I look at Jordan. He's doing great—it's *me* you need to worry about."

He asked what was wrong.

"Someone mistook me for Jordan's nanny at the park again," I said. "He's so fair that people think he's white. I was so fed up that I pulled out my breast and fed him right in front of that couple."

"Just put the little biscuit in the sun. He'll brown up."

As the weeks passed, we settled into a routine, which is to say that I knew what you needed by the sound of your cry and could count on you to wake up every two hours. (I timed my showers, naps, and phone calls accordingly.) But I was still not the picture of togetherness. I called your pediatrician so often with my new-mother questions that he must have thought I was insane. I brought page-long lists of questions to your check-ups: "Does his head seem big? Are you sure he's not color-blind? What about that red spot?"

Dr. Edelstein was incredibly patient, and it was a big day when the number of questions was in the single digits. I half expected him to reward me with a smiley face sticker.

When you were three months old, I took you to Los Angeles to see my sisters, Kim and Lynnette, and to have you baptized. Kim attended a small, multicultural Presbyterian church led by a young white pastor, the Reverend Howard Dodson, whom I admired. It would be his first christening.

Your aunts and I were having dinner at an Italian restaurant one evening when they commented on the unusual grunting sound you were making.

"He sounds like he's having trouble breathing," Lynnette said.

You seemed fine to me, and I worried that if I phoned your doctor one more time, he would stop returning my calls, so Lynnette suggested the "dial-a-nurse" service that my health insurer provided. We were in your aunt's car on our way to her house when I reached a nurse on my cell phone and explained your symptoms.

"That doesn't sound good at all," the woman said. "What you're describing might be respiratory distress."

Distress was the only word I needed to hear. In no time, Lynnette and I were speeding down the freeway toward the nearest emergency room. Perhaps sensing our agitation, you began crying.

"Maybe we should call the highway patrol for an escort," I wailed. "We're only two miles away!" Lynnette said, turning on her flashers instead to move traffic along.

We burst through the emergency room doors crying that we

had an infant in distress, whereupon a triage nurse assessed your vital signs: normal. A doctor examined you and ran tests. I rocked you anxiously until he returned with the results.

"Ma'am, there is nothing wrong with this baby. He has gas."

He gave me a brochure about colic and sent me to the billing office, where I paid what your aunt and I still refer to as "the gas bill."

"You did what?" Charles said, when he called my cell phone a few days later and I told him about our frantic emergency room expedition. "My poor son—I need to come home and rescue him."

"The nurse said 'distress.' Wouldn't you rather I be safe than sorry?"

"Yes, Ma, but you don't need to take him to the emergency room every time he burps."

"Fine, next time I'll let him suffer," I teased.

"No, you won't," Charles said, laughing.

I promised to send him pictures of you in your baptism outfit, an adorable white satin shorts suit with a bow tie and doves embroidered on the lapel.

Your father never questioned the decision to have you baptized without him, but I suspect he knew that I feared, down deep, that he could be killed, and I wanted him at least to have known that we had dedicated his son's life to God. Then he would know that even if he did not meet you on earth, he would see you someday in heaven.

The evening before the christening, I got a call from Dodson: there had been a change in plans, and what was supposed to be an intimate occasion would be anything but that. There had been a series of high-profile gang shootings in the neighborhood that week—shootings that left a teenage girl and boy dead. Dodson had hastily organized a reconciliation service for the families of the dead children, and it was scheduled for the same time as your baptism. (Apparently it was the only available time slot on the mayor's calendar.) Since you and I were returning to New York on Monday, we could not reschedule the christening.

It seemed like a macabre idea, but Dodson said that he envisioned the ceremony as a homecoming for those families, culminating with a celebration of life for ours.

Reluctantly, I agreed.

Television crews and half a dozen police cars were parked outside the church when we arrived, and armed police officers stood guard on the church lawn. The sanctuary, ordinarily spacious, was packed with people. I questioned my judgment in agreeing to baptize you under such conditions. What if the rival gang members who had killed those kids decided to drive by and shoot up the church?

I was still trying to decide whether to back out when something miraculous happened. I saw those other parents seized in sorrow and knew then that our place was in the sanctuary. I wanted to ease their suffering in any way that I could.

When it was time for us to make our way to the front of the church, I stood there swaying with you in my arms as the pastor placed a hand on your forehead, closed his eyes, and prayed. I looked at the mother of one of the dead gang members and wondered if she was thinking back to a time when her own child was still tiny and untouched by hatred and violence.

Pastor Dodson had told me that during the service I would have to literally hand you over to the members of the congregation so that they could welcome you into the church. When that time came, I instinctively offered you to that dead child's mother. She clutched you to her breast, shaking as she rocked you and wept. The brother of one of the victims, a boy of about sixteen, rubbed your head and kissed your cheek. Those strangers with whom we were suddenly connected passed you among themselves before someone placed you back in my arms. Tears flowed freely as you were welcomed into the church and christened as a child of God.

You squirmed when the minister sprinkled water on your head but otherwise remained silent and still. Then the congregation prayed for your father's protection and for your health and safety.

As the service concluded, so many people wanted to greet us that we stood in an impromptu receiving line accepting their hugs and good wishes. Mayor Antonio Villaraigosa held you and posed for pictures. An old Asian man with a creased face and white hair waited at the end of the line. When he finally made his way closer with an unsteady gait, he clutched my hand and smiled.

"God is pleased," he said, looking at me with tired eyes, and hobbled off.

This was salvation.

The healing you brought to those hurting people must have been what your father meant when he wrote to me after you were born: *I know he is a blessing to everyone who meets him.*

I am not sure why, but I never told your father about the reconciliation service that preceded your baptism. Perhaps I wanted to ignore the symbolism of it, representing as it did the tenuous thread between life and death. I tried to provide as idyllic an image as possible of your life during the months that remained until your father could come home—in case it was all he would ever experience of it.

Within weeks of the trip to Los Angeles we were on a plane again, flying to Kentucky to spend a weekend with both sets of your grandparents. It was important to me that you meet them, and for your father to see pictures of you with them. I was surprised at how sentimental I felt returning home as a mother for the first time. I had come of age in Radcliff, had kissed my first boyfriend there and learned to drive on those roads. Now my son would sleep under the same roof where I had grown into womanhood and met his father.

You met my father that day and he held you up and tickled your face with his gray beard—no longer the fearsome man who had raised me, but a gentle, rotund grandfather, the kind who passes out candy before dinner and gives rides on the back of his electric wheelchair. Arthritis had claimed his body and age had softened his heart. He still liked to lecture and to have the last word, but usually not when his grandchildren were speaking. Maybe you represented our second chance.

I took you out into the front yard and pointed out the spot where I had knocked over a bush when I was learning to drive and where I once played hopscotch. Then we walked under the towering oak tree that I had loved as a girl—the tree your dad and I had walked under the day we met.

I was sitting with you on the front porch when the Kings arrived the next morning. Your grandmother walked up the driveway with arms outstretched long before she was close enough to touch you.

"Just look at this baby," she beamed, rubbing her cheek against yours. Our two families were finally united. Even your aunt Gail, a lawyer in her mid-forties who was known as a fierce negotiator, softened when she took you into her arms. I did not know her well but she and I were both professional women with spunk and strong opinions, which might have been part of Charles's attraction to me.

The Kings took enough pictures to wallpaper a room and covered you with kisses when they left two days later. I also snapped dozens of pictures to send your father. He was so happy to receive them, especially the ones of you in his parents' arms. He told me he had been showing the pictures to his soldiers.

He wanted to know where I had gotten the Polo shirt and shorts you were wearing in the photos and how much weight you had gained. He asked if you were sleeping longer and wanted to know if I was still reading to you every day. I put the phone to your ear so he could speak to you and told him that you seemed to turn toward the sound of his voice. In those moments he was not simply a leader of men at war a world away—he was a father in love.

Eleven

Dear Jordan,

While I was writing to Charles in the spring of 2006 about your first smiles and the smell of your skin after a bath, he was writing to me about Iraqi children searching trash heaps for scraps of food to eat. He wrote of proudly watching American boys he had trained become men during battle, only to see them die in pools of blood in the streets in Iraq.

From the day your father and his soldiers crossed into Iraq from Kuwait, he realized that Operation Iraqi Freedom was different from any other conflict he had known. Instead of fighting at a distance, with missiles launched from ships and artillery rounds fired from tanks, U. S. soldiers engaged their elusive enemy in narrow, unfamiliar streets. He wrote to me about training Iraqi soldiers by day, never knowing whether they would join the insurgency by night.

You get fed up with the craziness and hatred. You really get tired of people trying to blow you up. Ma, this has been a long year. Our battalion lost ten soldiers. I take everything one day at a time and continue to pray.

I wondered how a man who knew he could be shot by an unseen adversary at any moment could ever reenter a world in which he was safe. I tried to focus on keeping his spirits up until his two-week leave, still several months away. I sent care packages stuffed with some of his favorite things: tuna, smoked nuts, Rice Krispie treats, and fitness magazines. I included cards scented with my perfume, my way of reminding him that he was adored.

There were times when my packages made things more difficult. In some of his letters, he wrote that the photographs and cards made him long even more for all that he was missing.

I'm sorry I couldn't be there for you during Jordan's birth. I missed a special occasion. He'll be a good 6 months old by the time I see him. I carry the pictures of him around in my cargo pocket and show them off. It's not a healthy practice because you have to stay focused at all times.

Much later, I would discover the details of your father's life in Iraq. I learned that Charles was a Death Dealer, as the roughly one thousand men of his heavy-tank, armor, and infantry battalion called themselves. As such, his survival depended on his ability to shut out thoughts of us. Formally the 1st Battalion, 67th Armored

Regiment, 2nd Brigade, 4th Infantry Division from Fort Hood, Texas, the Dealers operated in an area about thirty miles south of Baghdad—one of the most dangerous Sunni-Shiite fault lines. Iskandariyah, the town where the Dealers made their forward operating base, or FOB, was part of a larger region of about 2,700 square miles. Insurgents were everywhere. The military called it the Triangle of Death.

First Sergeant King, "Top," as his soldiers called him because of his rank, was in charge of the 105 men of Charlie Company—the Carnivores. He reported to a young West Point–trained commander named Stefan McFarland who was as ambitious as he was demanding. Captain McFarland, a tall, white, boyishly handsome former football player from Carrollton, Texas, was only twenty-nine but had considerable combat experience. He had served in Kuwait and was on his second tour of duty in Iraq.

Given his résumé and his gung-ho reputation, McFarland seemed destined to travel a straight line up the military chain of command. Charles sometimes referred to McFarland as "The Golden Boy," but he respected his command.

If the two men had taken different paths to military leadership, they shared a love for the institution and the company they led. While Charles had more experience, he considered the junior officer a competent leader who shared his high standards, and under their command the company became known for its willingness to take on tough missions.

"We were kind of famous," said Specialist Harold García, a proud Carnivore. "Charlie Company was the shit."

As first sergeant, Charles was Captain McFarland's go-to guy. Before the troops deployed, Charles oversaw their training for combat, making certain they could navigate a battlefield and operate sophisticated weapons. He also made certain that they knew something of the culture of Iraqi Muslims, both for defensive reasons and to avoid giving offense.

Charles would exercise with the weakest soldiers to improve their fitness and stamina. "When we went on company runs, he would go with us and smoke us sometimes," said Sergeant Adam Martínez, twenty-nine, a tanker in the unit. "It was uplifting for soldiers to see that a first sergeant could run us into the ground."

Leading his young soldiers tapped into Charles's paternal impulses and made him feel as if he were personally obligated to them. He even counseled the youngest soldiers about saving the first money they had ever earned. Their race, upbringing, religion, and politics didn't matter. What did was that every one of them had a family and a life to get back to. He would dedicate himself to their survival.

> *I was wondering how I was doing at my first sergeant*
> *position. God answered my prayer in a big way. The*
> *commander and I decided to have a get together with*
> *all the soldiers. We set aside a time where we could all*
> *get together and drink before we went to Iraq. Just*
> *about every soldier in the company came up to me and*
> *told me how much they appreciated me being their first*
> *sergeant. Thanks, God, I needed to hear that.*

Before he left, I asked your father to describe what a typical day in Iraq would entail. "Everything from making sure my soldiers get their mail to recovering their bodies," he said.

Given his gentleness at home, I was astounded to learn about

Charles's demeanor in the field. The first sergeant was a different person from my sweet, shy fiancé.

"He would get out there and yell his lungs out at us," Martínez told me. "He'd tear our heads off and stomp on us if we fucked up, but then he'd tell us, 'If you get in trouble, I'll come get you in the middle of the night.'"

Charles tearing people's heads off? I searched my mind for such an image.

As their leader, he would admonish his men before they headed out on missions to "stay alive and kill shit," which became Charlie Company's battle cry. I had never heard my Charles swear.

"I guess he was real good at turning on the switch and turning it off," Martínez said.

But Charles only yelled when he believed he had no other recourse, which is why his soldiers and superiors recall in great detail the times that he did. "He was an almost strikingly quiet, thoughtful leader," said Lieutenant Colonel Patrick Donahoe, Charles's battalion commander. "Here was a guy who looked like some Greek statue. He had the physical presence, so he didn't have to talk loud and didn't have to always shout at guys. He had this kind, calm demeanor to him that soldiers just responded to."

It was precisely because Charles and McFarland were such superior leaders that their Charlie Company saw the most combat action in the battalion. "I told them what that meant for them is that they get the most difficult missions we had in Iraq and they would get the most dangerous areas we had in Iraq," Donahoe said. "Those guys were war fighters. They were the guys who could figure out how to get to their objectives when, given the same set of circumstances, other companies would not. If I was going to send anybody up there, I had to send a unit that was cohesive enough that, if it came to it, they could take the losses and take the everyday grind of going in there. And I had to have a unit where the individual soldiers were confident in their leadership."

The Dealers' mission was to locate and destroy insurgency cells, train local military and security forces, and help transfer the region to Iraqi control. Achieving that goal required as much diplomacy as armaments. So the Dealers worked to broker peace deals between Sunni and Shiite factions. They protected the construction site of a new police station in a small, volatile town not ten miles from their base, Jurf as-Sakhr. Insurgents had blown up the last one. They whitewashed schools, oversaw the installation of water purification systems, and built marketplaces for local merchants to sell their wares. But before the battalion could work on the governance and goodwill efforts, Charlie Company had to pave the way with a far more arduous task.

"An awful lot of killing had to be done before we could do that," Donahoe said. "Charlie Company was down there in the knife fight, if you will, rooting out a very well-entrenched insurgency."

Within a month of Team Carnivore's arrival, civilians and insurgents alike had felt its presence. The soldiers had seized large caches of weapons and commandeered an enemy encampment they called "Carnivore Island": a one-story concrete house surrounded not by water but by desert. It got its name because of its isolation, rather than its proximity to the Euphrates River.

Word spread quickly among the locals about how the Carnivores had transformed the Island. Before they took it over, it had been the site of what the *New York Times* called "a clandestine court," where, according to Iraqi police, "insurgent judges would try, torture and execute collaborators." Thereafter, it became a patrol base from which the company conducted surveillance of the region and launched attacks on insurgents.

"That was an enemy sanctuary where we found thousands of pounds of explosives," McFarland said. "Taking over the house put us in their backyard, so the big, bad Americans were in there now and the enemy had to face it."

The position also put the American soldiers in good stead with the locals. In an area that had known constant fighting as the warring Sunnis and Shiites looted merchants and killed locals caught in their crosshairs, the soldiers added a measure of security.

There was, however, a tactical downside to making this the company's patrol base: the ten-mile route between the Island and the battalion's forward operating base in Iskandariyah. It was a perilous sliver of asphalt known as Route Patty, not more than a lane and a half wide and littered with deadly IEDs, or improvised explosive devices.

"Everyone knows that it was pretty much IED alley," Martínez said. Charles called it "one of the most dangerous roads we have." He had even discussed the dangers with his "battle buddy," First Sergeant Arenteanis "Tony" Jenkins, who was his bunkmate in Iraq and led another company in the battalion.

"Everybody had an uneasy feeling about that road," Tony told me. "There were so many blind spots coming around curves with a bunch of trees, and what you were trying to look for was a tree out of place. One time we halted a convoy because we noticed that a tree wasn't there a week before." Trees often contained camouflaged wires attached to detonators. A wire mistaken for a twig could be deadly.

The explosives that lay in wait for the Americans were as crude as they were lethal. They could be deceptively small when hidden inside a soda can, or as large as a discarded crate at the side of the road. They could be packed into propane canisters, disguised in rubbish, or tucked into a briefcase in an abandoned car. The bomb makers were creative and audacious—sometimes mockingly so. They even hid IEDs in discarded MRE (meals ready to eat) packages.

Making an IED required only a rudimentary knowledge of explosives. All the insurgents needed was a combustible substance (usually gunpowder, dynamite, or a mixture of hydrogen peroxide, gasoline, and nitrate) along with nails, metal, glass, and rocks, all of which were crammed into the container. The bomb makers often used nine-volt batteries as power sources and triggered the explosives with detonators fashioned from common electronic devices. A cell phone or car alarm could serve as a bomb trigger. Even the remote control for a toy would do.

Sometimes, under the cover of darkness, the insurgents dug craters in the road, placed explosives in them, and repacked the asphalt. After they scattered dirt around the area, the road looked untouched, especially from atop a tank. The enemy also hid bombs in the carcasses of dogs and other animals, which were then placed along the road.

It was on the treacherous Route Patty that Charles would look not just for bombs but Iraqi children, who would stand at the side of the road and marvel at the American convoys.

"He'd say to his gunner, 'Are my kids out there?'" Tony recalled. "He took candy out there to those kids all the time. He thought if he could make a difference or have one smile, just by throwing people candy, why not do it? He didn't look at it like some soldiers did, that these were little Iraqis growing up to be big Iraqis who were going to kill Americans."

But it was on Route Patty that Charlie Company also experienced its most crushing defeats.

*The first of May we lost our first soldier. It was very
sad. Everyone cared about Cpl. Robbie Light. We had
a get-together the night before the memorial so that
everyone could have a chance to speak about how he
lived. The soldiers had some of the wildest stories to
tell about Robbie. We laughed and smiled, thinking
about the crazy things he would do to make us laugh.
That was a healing night, a chance to say farewell to a
fallen soldier. Laughter is great medicine for the soul.*

Corporal Robbie Light was just twenty-one years old. His wife
was pregnant with their first child, a daughter.

Charles was so shaken after he recovered Robbie's body that he
mailed the journal to me immediately, even though it still had about
a dozen empty pages, in case he never made it back. Charles also
seemed to need to tell me about Robbie's death. In a letter he wrote:

*I know you have heard the bad news. It was something
I hoped I would not have to experience. It has been
a rough two months. This week has been the most
painful thus far. I can't begin to tell you. Today is a
tough day for my company. We had a memorial
for one of my soldiers killed in action. I'm dealing with
it; you would be proud of me. It's hard talking on the
phone. You can't say everything you want to say
because of all of the restrictions.*

Yes, we have been in a lot of pain lately. Everyone in the battalion has been supportive. I will be glad when this week is over.

I knew when my soldiers came to my room and knocked on my door that night that I would have to face the inevitable. Would I be able to handle it was the question. Don't worry, Ma. I did above and beyond. The memorial was the toughest, but we pulled through and gave our fallen comrade a good send off.

Don't you worry about me, Ma, I have a great company. We will keep the memory of our friend with us as we continue on with our missions.

He would have said all this to me on the phone, but the military restricted what we could discuss. Once, when I was venting about "stop loss," the government's practice of adding another tour of duty for soldiers who were about to be discharged, the line suddenly went dead. Your father called back and told me not to say anything like that or we would once again be cut off.

I could feel Charles's anguish in what he wrote about Robbie, and it distressed me that I could not be there to comfort him. I could not wrap him in my embrace and whisper for him to hold on until the pain subsided. Nor could I call him to try to raise his spirits. Even the letter I wrote would take weeks to reach him.

I knew that Charles's 104 remaining soldiers were drawing on his strength during those bleak days, but I wondered who was giving *him* strength. Then I remembered the angel print. His faith would see him through, I thought, just as his love for his Biscuit would sustain him.

"Oh, man, that was his life, right there," García told me. "He loved that little boy. He always carried a picture in this book he had." Charles's bunkmate, Tony, often noticed that Charles's light was on late into the night. It was then, he thinks, that your father was writing to you in his journal.

Tony and Charles had known each other casually before they deployed and shared a bond as black first sergeants. But it was only when they lived together in Iraq in their cramped cinder-block, wood, and canvas quarters that they discovered that they had a great deal more in common. Both had lived in Mobile, Alabama. Both were athletic and liked to run. Both were engaged to marry when their tours were over.

"With us being first sergeants we couldn't associate with the lower enlisted members and we didn't associate with the officers, so the only person we could really associate with was a first sergeant," said Tony, a lanky, high-energy forty-six-year-old.

Charles and his roommate looked out for each other. If one of them was late coming in from a mission and the dining facility was closing, the other would save a plate of food for his buddy. They had promised that if either got hurt in battle, the other would come to the rescue no matter what the personal risk. And there was one other promise they made to each other. I'll tell you about that later.

Your father confided in other friends, too, about his plans for a life with the two of us. His buddy Sergeant First Class Helder Camera knew of our relationship from their days as tankers at Fort Riley, a time when he would teasingly ask your father at the end of a workweek where he was headed. "I'm flying to see my girl," Charles would say.

When Charles e-mailed Camera, who was serving in another part of Iraq, to say that he was getting married, his buddy was shocked. "At Riley he said he was never going to get married again," Camera told me.

Camera wrote back congratulating Charles and confided that he was having family problems. "I know you love the military," Charles e-mailed back, "but one day you are going to retire and the people at the end of the tunnel waiting for you will be your family."

Charles and I had talked about getting married on a Caribbean cruise a few months after he returned, inviting only our families and a few friends. In the weeks after he left, I thought planning the wedding would be the ideal way to keep him focused on coming home. I pictured myself sending him fabric swatches and sample invitations. I leafed through bridal magazines, fantasizing about a gown—off-white, simple, elegant, and formfitting. Naturally, I would be svelte. I would carry a bouquet with tropical flowers. Since I have always been clumsy, and since Charles had minimal rhythm, I wondered how I could talk him into dance lessons. Could I send cake samples to Iraq?

But I never got far with my planning. It all felt wrong, inappropriate even. I could not bring myself to commit to caterers or florists—much less buy a dress—while my man was still in harm's way. I abandoned the idea after a few months.

Instead, I concentrated on losing my remaining baby weight in time for our wedding. Mostly my fitness strategy involved long walks pushing your stroller, since I could not seem to drag myself to the gym in our building. I wondered how Charles found the fortitude to start his days in the gym in Iraq. Even his soldiers marveled at his discipline.

"It was hard over there, it really was," said one of them, Sergeant First Class Kenny Morris. "I spent six out of every nine days outside the gate, so the two or three days inside the gate I didn't waste my time going to the gym. I chose to relax, but he was obviously very physically fit and took a lot of pride in keeping himself in shape. I know he also ran a lot."

Charles did not exercise out of vanity. It was a form of therapy. It also gave him the stamina to do his job. Sergeant Shoan Mohammed, a gunner in your father's unit, recalled walking for miles with Charles in full body armor in the dry heat, searching for weapons and combatants in areas that were not easily reachable by vehicle. When the soldiers took breaks and sat down, Charles was always the first up. "That was to let the guys know that if he could do it, we could do it, too," Mohammed told me.

Lt. Col. Donahoe recalled one such mission, during which dozens of his soldiers became dehydrated. "It was hot as the dickens. We had to give fifty to seventy IVs." Charles, he said, was not one of the soldiers treated. "He wouldn't have allowed anyone to give him one anyway. The first sergeant was not going to let himself get to the point where he had to let his guys see him get an IV."

Your father was so determined to set an example for his troops that he often made a point of taking on duties usually left to a private or another entry-level soldier, dedication that occasionally took his soldiers by surprise. One day, after a mission to a village to scout out insurgents, Mohammed was "out in the middle of nowhere," surrounded by sand, when he saw a tank approaching. The gun loader, typically the junior soldier riding the tank, began waving at him to come toward him.

"I gave him the finger, not thinking anything of it, for him calling me over there as if I didn't have anything better to do," Mohammed admitted. "So this loader jumps off the tank, I mean literally jumps off the hatch, and now he's really mad coming toward me. When I started walking toward him I realized it was First Sergeant King and said 'Oh shit, what did I just do?' I'm five-six and a half and about a buck and a half dripping wet, and he's about six-two and two hundred fifty pounds. He was walking through two feet of sand."

When your father reached his soldier, he got in his face. "Don't you ever give me the finger again," he barked.

Charles cooled down quickly, though. He realized that Mohammed had not recognized him from so far away. And how many first sergeants performed the duties of a gun loader?

"You can always humble yourself to do the job at the bottom is what he told me," Mohammed said. "To me, his rank and stature wasn't what I respected him for. I respected him as a man. There was a selflessness in him."

Charles did not always hold his soldiers to the standard he set for himself. He had a soft streak. One of his soldiers' wives, Valerie Lauer, recalled how Charles pretended not to notice when she spent several nights in the men's barracks in Fort Hood with her husband, Timothy, before they moved into their home. "I even got to climb into a tank," she told me.

One soldier recalled how Charles gave him time off from combat training to be with his wife for the birth of their baby. "He gave me his word that I could go and he kept his promise. I stayed in the hospital three days because she had a C-section and he didn't ask once when I was going to come back to formation."

These stories were difficult to hear. On one hand, I was envious; Charles had not always been as generous with us as he had been with his men. On the other, I loved him more for embracing the responsibilities of his position in a way that set him apart. Only about 10 percent of enlisted troops ever attain the rank of first sergeant. Fewer still lead troops in war. Charles also earned an army Combat Action Badge for "engaging the enemy" in battle. He was awarded the badge for his actions during a gun battle that took place less than three months after he arrived in Iraq. Some men from another company were ambushed and your father drove into the melee and pulled the wounded to safety. "Without regard to his personal safety, he remained in the kill zone to ensure the rapid and safe evacuation of every other soldier," reads the citation nominating him for the badge.

Charles did not care much about medals and awards, but he did give and demand respect for men and women in uniform.

> *The 18th was a long, solemn night. We had a memorial for two soldiers (from another company) who were killed by an improvised explosive device. None of my soldiers went to the memorial. Their excuse was that they didn't want to go because it was depressing. I told them it was selfish of them not to pay their respects to two men who were selfless in giving their lives for their country.*
>
> *Things may not always be easy or pleasant for you, that's life, but always pay your respect for the way people lived and what they stood for.*
>
> *It's the honorable thing to do.*

I could tell from the letters Charles wrote in the weeks just before his leave that the trauma of combat was wearing on him. After all, he had been away for nearly eight months. I began to make plans for his homecoming. I bought a black leather backpack for him to use as a diaper bag. I stocked the refrigerator with his favorite beer. I did not know if my efforts would help, but I would have done anything to soothe the suffering I read in those letters.

I can't bring myself to write about some of my experiences here. I guess after a while you become numb to what's been going on or what can happen to you. Had some frustrating days and frightening nights. Soon they will all end when we get home.

Tell Jordan not to grow up too quickly. Daddy will be home soon.

Twelve

Dear Jordan,

I carried you under my heart for the better part of a year and nursed you for just as long. I got up in the middle of the night to make sure you were breathing. When you cried I patted you, burped you, rocked you, and sang to you. But all your father had to do was walk in the front door that August day and you instantly loved him.

Your dad had worried that he would be a stranger to you, and that two weeks would not be long enough for you to bond with him. I guess God knew your time together would be brief.

What I had worried about was how Charles would handle the transformation from first sergeant to father. It had been a long journey and I wanted his homecoming to be perfect. So the day before he was due to arrive, I cooked while you slept, making what I had learned from reading the journal was his favorite meal:

> *My favorite meal is honestly chicken, cooked either fried or baked, with candied yams, greens or green*

> *beans, and corn bread. That meal always puts a smile on my face.*
>
> *Your grandparents are from the South, so I got the taste for southern cooked food from them. Grandma King's mother could bake the best sweet potato pie ever. She passed away with the recipe but I still remember how great they tasted.*

It took half a dozen calls to my mother to prepare the yams and two to my sister for the greens. The chicken was another issue entirely.

I had been a vegetarian for fifteen years, so trying to clean that dead bird made me gag. I had made Cornish hens for Charles for Thanksgiving, but they were tiny little things that did not require much preparation. The chicken, though, was squishy and a sick shade of yellow. I poked at it and rolled it over but could not bring myself to actually handle the thing. Thank goodness for Shaika, my cleaning lady. She was watching, amused, from the living room and noticed my distress.

"Need some help?" she asked in her Caribbean accent.

"No, I'm okay," I lied.

"Are you sure?"

"Well, if you really don't mind. I've never cut up a chicken."

She ran water in the sink and sliced the chicken under it. She filled a pan with vinegar and water and let the pieces soak while she scavenged my spice rack for seasonings. I watched her dunk a breast and then a drumstick into a bowl of flour. She heated the frying oil and set the pieces in the skillet.

"You have no idea how much this means to me," I told her.

She said she was doing it for my soldier, then offered to stay in case you woke up before I had time to finish the rest of the meal and take a shower. I pulled the cornbread out of the oven and stirred my greens, then hopped quickly in and out of the shower.

My body had bounced back pretty well from the pregnancy, but it was still a struggle to squeeze into the pair of black jeans that, pre–baby fat, had hugged my hips and shaped my legs nicely. I chose a rose-colored blouse lined with black lace that showed off my newly plump breasts. After a quick makeup application and a spray of perfume, I set the table for dinner and sent Shaika on her way with a huge hug. Charles's plane was due to arrive in half an hour. You were awake by then, so I dressed you in a one-piece striped blue outfit, sat you on my lap, and waited.

Two hours later, Charles still had not arrived, and I had begun to panic. Had he inadvertently given me his flight information in *Baghdad* time? I realized that he must have. That meant he would not be home until the following day! I felt like crying.

I could not sit in our apartment any longer, so I put you in your stroller and the food in the refrigerator. We went for a long walk on the longest day of my life.

It was not until the light of the next morning, when Charles called from Atlanta, that I could breathe more deeply. He was on U.S. soil.

I told him about my confusion the day before and he said he was sorry.

"It's not your fault," I said. "I just hope you don't mind leftover chicken."

You and I spent the afternoon in the park, where I watched so many dads pushing strollers and swings. I had waited a long time for yours to be among them.

Finally, Charles called from LaGuardia. He was on his way

home. I had instructed our doorman to ring our apartment when Charles was in the elevator. When he did, I jumped, nervous and giddy at once. I smoothed my hair and our clothes, then stood in the doorway.

When I saw Charles walking toward us in his uniform, for a moment I could not breathe. He smiled broadly and dropped his duffle bag.

"Hello, Daddy. Come meet your son," I said, placing you in your father's arms. It was a moment I will never forget. He smothered you in a hug and then released one arm to pull me into the embrace. He kissed me and squeezed us tighter. We laughed. You looked startled.

Then your dad studied your face and hands and looked into your eyes, just as I had done for the first time six months earlier. He held you close and breathed in your scent, just as I had.

"He's beautiful," Charles said, as you squirmed.

> *The first time I laid eyes on you, you were everything your mother described. You certainly charm people with those beautiful blue eyes.*
>
> *Son, you are an African American. Always be proud of who you are. You will be challenged because of your complexion and the color of your eyes. Let your character and deeds shine in everything you do.*

Outwardly, Charles looked like the same man he was the last time I saw him, only thinner and a deeper shade of brown. He had shaved his head, and the mustache I loved was gone, but his smile was as beautiful as ever, and so were his bright eyes.

I watched as he gazed at you as though you were the most amazing thing he had ever seen. He touched your soft hair and then asked for his bag. He had brought presents, a stuffed camel for you and a stone figure of a mother and child for me.

Charles went into the bedroom and lay on his back on our bed, raising you in the air above him. You looked down and giggled as though the two of you had played that way before. It made your father laugh, too—the sweet music of two beautiful voices in harmony. I stood silently at the foot of the bed, arms folded. Even if there had been words to describe how I was feeling, they would have simply gotten in the way.

Finally, the burden I had felt ever since your father left was lifted. I no longer had to pretend to myself that the stabbing sensation I felt every time the phone rang was just indigestion. I did not have to worry that he might not receive the latest pictures of you in time, did not have to dread the nights I reached for him in my sleep and awoke in agony.

It was too early to tell what Charles was feeling or how the war had worn on him. All that mattered at that moment was that we were at peace in our little safety zone. I thought of all the tomorrows we would have with your father—fourteen to begin with, and then a lifetime more. There would be time in the years ahead for making sandcastles and putting up Christmas trees, for playing tooth fairy and tossing footballs. Yet I was greedy: I wanted each second to last an hour, each hour a day.

Charles seemed suspended in time, too, until he suddenly stood up and walked back into the living room carrying you. His mood had changed; he seemed agitated and had a panicked expression on his face. He said his stomach ached and asked if I had antacids. He searched in his bag for an inhaler.

Was he sick, or could it be an anxiety attack? I calmly lifted you out of his arms, gave him an antacid, and ran a warm bath as he breathed in the mist from the inhaler. I also brought him a beer, thinking it might help him relax. Charles was allergic to shellfish but I had never known him to have respiratory problems. As I watched him settle into the tub, I wondered what had caused his new shortness of breath.

"Sweetie, we'll stay here and keep you company," I said and sat on the closed toilet seat with you in my arms. "Just relax."

Charles exhaled deeply, took a long drink of his beer, and closed his eyes. I thought of turning on music but was afraid the sound or my sudden movement might startle him. Instead I sat quietly as he opened his eyes and looked up at us. He cupped his hands full of water and let it fall onto his face and chest.

"Tell me about your inhaler," I said softly.

"Oh, I have asthma," he said.

"How long have you had it?"

"We live by a power plant. I guess I got it there."

I was struck by two things. First, he had said that he "lived" near a power plant, just as he had given me his flight arrival in Baghdad time. How extraordinary that the mind can be conditioned to imagine home as being any place that becomes familiar, even one of the most treacherous places on earth. Charles's very survival must have depended on him immersing himself in that alien environment, so that he was not paralyzed by fear or overcome with longing for the place where he really belonged.

The other thing was his certainty that he had become asthmatic. There was no way to know what he had been inhaling near that plant, but it seemed to me just as likely that his breathing difficulties were a reaction to the stress of combat. Since he was a leader, there were few opportunities to express his fear. Perhaps he kept it inside until it became so powerful that he had to release it, somehow.

I asked him whether the military doctors had actually diagnosed him with asthma, and he said they had. I offered to take him
to my doctor for a second opinion.

"I'm fine, Ma. The inhaler works," he said.

I did not want to upset him so I decided to wait and suggest it
again after his tour of duty was over.

Charles got out of the tub, looking much more relaxed, and
again lay down with you on the bed. I went into the kitchen to prepare a plate of food and Charles must have smelled it because he
came into the living room holding you and said that he could not
eat. He seemed exhausted.

"I'm going to take the baby for a walk so you can get some rest,"
I told him. "But please try to at least nibble on some cornbread. I'll
bring you chicken noodle soup."

I had expected the man I met at the door to be somehow different from the one who had walked out of it all those months ago.
But I had not expected his suffering to show so soon. What he had
seen and done over there I could not imagine. But there was clearly
no way to emerge from a world in which you are routinely involved
in taking and saving lives and not be transformed. I would try to
lighten his burden while he was home, but then he would have to
return and endure more of whatever he had been through.

Your father was still asleep when we returned from our walk
late that afternoon. You were taking a nap yourself, snug in your
stroller. I left you in the living room and snuck quietly into the bedroom. Ever clumsy, I knocked over a candleholder on the dresser
and he bolted upright.

"Dana, are you all right?" he shouted.

I put my arms around him, looked into his eyes.

"I'm fine and so are you," I said. "You're home now, and you're
safe."

For the first time since he arrived, we kissed ravenously, like the lovers we had been.

"You've been there for me for as long as I've known you, even when I didn't deserve it. Now it's my turn to take care of you," I said softly. "I love you, baby."

He held me so tight it almost hurt, then released me and looked into my face.

"I love you, too, Dana" was all he said.

He would not eat more than a few bites of cornbread and a sip of broth. Then I suggested that he help me with your bath. He undressed you and studied your plump little body, remarking on your chubby knees and long feet. When I half filled your little blue tub on the kitchen counter, your dad watched as you looked startled for a moment before relaxing in the warm water. He watched as I washed your face and hair and then your squirming body. I dried you off and he rubbed lotion on you. I dressed you in a yellow sleeper and sat in a chair in the living room feeding you. Your father was mesmerized by the sight of me nursing his son. His healing had begun.

The warm bath and your full stomach made you drowsy and we laid you in bed between us. You lifted your head and looked at your father and, I will never forget it, a wide smile spread across your face. Then you went to sleep.

Charles took your tiny hand in his and rubbed it. He rubbed your hair and kissed your cheek, staring at you as though he was afraid to even blink for fear of missing a detail.

After a shower, I rubbed baby oil on my body, sprayed myself with perfume, and slipped into a sheer pink nightgown. I was not sure what the night would bring, but I wanted to feel soft and sexy in his arms anyway.

When I returned, I put you in your crib, then got in bed beside

Charles. He took me into his arms and kissed me wildly, lifting my nightgown over my head and letting himself rediscover my body. Then he made love to me with a force that startled me. He tried to be tender, but there was a rawness to his longing. It was as if he had been holding on just to make it back to me and release all his pain.

We were asleep but still clinging to each other when you awoke later that night, crying in the darkness. Your father instantly got out of bed and changed your diaper, then handed you to me and watched as I nursed you in the moonlit room. After you fell asleep, he lifted you out of my arms and kissed your cheek before lowering you back into your crib. Then my Charles returned to our bed.

"I'm hungry, too," he whispered in my ear.

Sometime in the twilight hours I opened my eyes and found Charles staring at me. "Why are you looking at me like that?" I asked.

"I like to wake up and watch you sleep," he said. "I always have."

I felt an overpowering passion for this man who would leave again so soon. I hugged him as tight as I could and felt milk trickle down my chest and onto his. He held on, too, so tight it hurt, and it somehow seemed we still could not get close enough. I could barely breathe, but I did not care. My man was home, safely in my arms.

We awoke slowly the next morning and lounged in bed sipping coffee—a normal Sunday for an ordinary family. No bombs would be exploding in Charles's world that day.

Your dad lay in bed reading to you while I took what might have been the longest shower of my life. I had never been so glad to see wrinkles on my fingers. You were still content by your father's side when I returned to the bedroom wearing a towel.

"Hey, do I get an honorary membership in your gentlemen's

club?" I said. "I can't believe this boy has taken to you so quickly. Do you know how many diapers I've changed and how many times I've whipped out my boobs to feed him?"

"Hey man, what do you think? Should we let her in our club?" Charles asked you.

It was nearly noon before we made our way out the door. I tried to convince Charles to stop at a deli for breakfast. "At least some toast," I pleaded. But he still insisted that he had no appetite.

We strolled through a park looking out onto the East River, Charles pushing your stroller and my hand rubbing his back. Every few minutes he stopped to make sure the sunshade was still shielding your face. We sat on a bench and watched people jog and walk dogs and toss Frisbees. Things people do in a peaceful place.

A helicopter flew overhead and the sound made Charles flinch. He pulled out his inhaler and breathed in the medicine. I waited for him to speak.

"You know what I was just thinking about?" he eventually said. "All the soldiers who won't be around to watch their children grow up."

"We have to count our blessings that you're not one of them," I said.

He would only have six weeks left in Iraq when he returned, and then he would be home for good.

"Charles, you just have to get through the end of this. It's almost over, and this little guy needs his daddy."

He beamed at you.

"I need you, too," I said.

"I know," he said, and then: "So what do you want for Christmas, Ma?"

"You home."

"We have to do something special," Charles insisted. "It'll be

Jordan's first Christmas. I hope you can take some time off. Maybe we can take him on a carriage ride in Central Park."

"It's a date."

As the week went on, I could see the mellow man I had known emerging. Noises no longer startled him. He ate skinless chicken and salad. He still barely put you down.

We headed into the subway one afternoon to take care of the only bit of business on our agenda—correcting your birth certificate. Charles had taken the news of my dust-up at the hospital calmly and wanted to do what was necessary to get it fixed. But when we entered the Office of Vital Records, my spirits sank. Dozens of people were in line, waiting to approach clerks sitting behind glass partitions in what looked like bank teller booths. We filled out a form while we waited and asked strangers in line to sign as witnesses. When we finally made it to one of the windows, I explained our situation to the clerk.

"Put your form in that slot," the young woman said, unyielding. She looked as if she had heard every manner of paternity story and was simply waiting for quitting time.

"But isn't there someone we can talk to? He has to go back to Iraq soon."

"No, there's no manager on duty," she said brusquely.

I gave up and slipped our form into the slot, hoping for the best. Then we stepped away from the window and I asked your dad to stop a minute.

"Charles, I hope this will take care of it but, if it doesn't, I swear to you that I'll see to it that your name is added to Jordan's birth certificate. I'm just so sorry it's not on the original." I wanted him to hear me make that promise aloud.

"Thanks, Ma. I know you'll take care of it."

As we left the building, Charles was enjoying strolling through the downtown city streets and I did not want to spoil his mood with my anger. But inside I was seething. How could it be that no one—not the Congress, the military, hospital administrators—had dealt with the issue of birth certificates for children born to single military fathers away at war? It was a grave injustice that a blank should appear where a father's name should be simply because he was in combat when his baby was born. That a marriage license was the only way to avoid the problem was insulting. Worst of all, no one seemed to care.

I was hosting a baby shower for your father that evening, but we had the whole afternoon in front of us, and spent most of it relaxing while you napped. Before I knew it, the clock said 4:00 p.m. Our guests were arriving at 5:30 and I had not even done the grocery shopping, let alone prepare the food. Charles rushed out to the grocery while I fed and bathed you, running back and forth from the kitchen every time the musical mobile on your playpen stopped and you began to wail. I was still wearing sweat pants and a T-shirt when he returned, and was in the process of wiping dribble off my shirt. He smiled and gazed at my lips—an amorous look I knew well.

"Charles, *again*? Are you kidding? I know you've been stuck in the desert with a bunch of men for nine months, but we have guests arriving in less than an hour."

We were barely dressed when the first guests arrived—Lara, who worked for me, and Ciro, my gay Italian friend, who had a crush on Charles. The two of them pushed past me to your father, hugging him tightly and telling him how good he looked. As more guests arrived, I watched each of them take your father into long, warm embraces. People were taking pictures, giggling, watching him hold you. I realized the evening was not about what I served; it was about sustenance for our spirits. I gave up on cooking and ordered pizza.

It was, after all, a baby shower, so someone ordered Charles to sit in a chair in the middle of the room and open his gifts. I could tell he was embarrassed. He handed you to me, the first time during the evening that you left his arms. He unwrapped some books about fatherhood, a set of tub toys, and a small photo album to fill with pictures from his leave that he could take back to Iraq. He opened my gifts last: a coffee mug with his favorite picture of you and the black leather backpack, which I had filled with diapers and wet wipes, pacifiers and burp cloths.

Charles was not the type to make speeches but he made sure to spend time with each guest. Several times I heard him talking about his soldiers.

"I just hope everybody's all right when I get back," he said. "They know it's almost time to come home, so I have to work hard to keep them focused."

Lara and Miriam wanted to discuss the politics of the war, but Charles mostly smiled and listened. Katti kissed his cheek and told him she had been lifting him up in prayer.

"Don't you worry about your family," she said. "I've got your back."

You fell asleep at sunset, but laughter and your hunger woke you a few hours later. I sat near a window surrounded by friends, rocking you back to sleep. Your father was standing at the edge of the room; he seemed lost in his thoughts. I caught his eye and motioned for him to sit beside me, but he just stood there, watching— savoring the love that filled the room. We ended the night with promises to our friends of an even bigger celebration when your father returned for good. After the final guest left around midnight, your father and I stood in the living room, hugging in silence and gazing out the window for the longest time.

I realized as we settled into bed that night that Charles had not used his inhaler that day. He was eating much more and had resumed ironing my clothes in the mornings.

"I think we need a mommy day tomorrow," he said as I lay in his arms.

"That's not necessary," I said. "I'm supposed to be taking care of you, remember?"

Charles stood firm. "Jordan and I are going to take you to get a massage. And then he and I are going to hang out."

"Hang out where?"

"We'll go to the park and the bookstore. Just leave me enough milk and diapers."

I reluctantly agreed. "But I'm going to keep my cell phone near in case you need me," I said.

I awoke in the middle of the night with full breasts and pumped the milk he would need for his first father-son outing. Charles offered to keep me company. So he sat next to me in the bathroom and we talked about our perfect baby.

"He looks like you, you know," Charles said.

"I see you in him, too."

"Dana, this boy will be a blessing to everyone he meets. He's special. Remember that I said that."

We fell asleep listening to you breathe in the crib nearby.

A light rain was falling the next morning—sleeping weather.

When I'm with your mother I always liked it when it rained in New York City. Boy could I relax, just listening to the raindrops hitting the window. We would stay at home and read and cuddle.

The rain had dwindled to a mist by early afternoon, and your father bundled you in blankets in your stroller and put the rain cover over it. We walked to a spa that I liked in our neighborhood and he followed me inside, handing the woman at the front desk his credit card and urging me to get a massage, a facial, a manicure, and anything else I wanted.

"Just a massage," I said. The attention made me blush.

Peeking through the window as the two of you left, I watched your dad push your stroller down the street, wearing his new backpack. Then I wrapped myself in a luxurious robe and sipped water flavored with slices of lemon while I waited for the massage therapist, who led me into a candlelit room. I had just about succeeded in willing myself to relax when the hour-long treatment was over.

Your father arrived precisely when he said he would and I watched him maneuver your stroller through the front door as though he had been doing it for months. He had changed your diaper twice, he said, and fed and burped you. He showed me the books he had bought for you and said that you had charmed the women in the checkout line.

"You should have seen him, flirting with those women," Charles bragged. "The cashiers kept trying to get people to move up in the line but they were surrounding us, talking about how cute he was. One woman chased me down the street to tell me his sock was falling off."

"I don't think I'm letting the two of you out of my sight again," I teased, imagining my men surrounded by gorgeous, indulgent women.

"Blame your son."

It might have been his ease with you that day that emboldened me to share with him an idea that I had—that he could take early retirement after he came home and care for you full-time for a couple of years while I worked. He seemed slightly taken aback by the proposal.

"Dana, you know you're not the type of woman to be married to a man who doesn't work, and I'm not the type of man to not take care of my family."

I told him he *would* be taking care of our family—and, in a way, still contributing financially given the astronomical cost of New York child care. I told him he could work on his art and teach—or do whatever he wanted as a second career—when you started school.

"So many black kids grow up without fathers," I said. "It would be nice if ours had a daddy who was the primary caretaker. And you have nothing to prove about your work ethic."

He said he would consider it—but I knew that for a man as old-fashioned as Charles, the notion was radical.

I had planned to make a simple salad for lunch and save my appetite for our time alone that night at our favorite Mexican restaurant while you stayed home with a babysitter. But your father suggested that we make it a family lunch instead of a dinner date. He didn't want to be without you for even a few hours. So we hailed a cab and took you along on our date.

As we gazed at you cooing in your baby carrier, we agreed that we did not need an evening out alone to reconnect romantically.

"I think we've already taken care of that," I said.

He smiled at me bashfully and fed me a salsa-dipped tortilla chip.

"So when do you want to get married?" Charles asked.

I told him I had picked the perfect date: June 9, a Saturday— the day that fell between my birthday on June 8 and his on June 10. He loved that idea.

I asked what he thought of our original plan to get married on a cruise ship and invite our families along. We could have a reception in New York when we got back.

"You just had my baby, so you get whatever you want," he said.

"I guess I should start looking for a dress."

"Then I guess I better look for a tuxedo."

"No," I said emphatically. "Anyone can wear a tux. I'm marrying a soldier. Nothing would make me prouder than to walk down the aisle and see you in your military dress blues."

Charles grinned.

I asked what he wanted to do the next day. He could think of only one thing: buying winter clothes for you.

"You want to buy winter clothes in August?"

He nodded. I did not ask why.

We had not been shopping together since I was pregnant and it felt nice doing it again as new parents. The winter merchandise had begun to arrive, and Charles filled a cart with jackets and mittens and long-sleeved shirts and cotton sweat suits, as well as socks and diapers and a larger baby tub. He kept asking whether you needed anything else and I kept saying you did not.

He was simply being a dutiful dad, I told myself. But I couldn't help feeling concerned about why he was thinking so far ahead. Was he planning for a future that didn't include himself?

"Dana, I want to write you a check," he said when we got home. "I want you to have half of my combat pay."

I resisted. We still had some of the checks he had given me. He reminded me that I would be going back to work and would need to pay for your babysitter.

"I'm not taking half your combat pay," I insisted.

"Dana, please. It's for our son. And you should buy something for yourself, too."

He wrote a check and tried to hand it to me. I waved him away.

"Take it, Dana," he said. Finally, I did.

Then Charles began to talk about life insurance. I began to pace.

"Charles, if something happened to you, you know I would only use that money to take care of Jordan."

He put his hands on my shoulders, his expression as serious as I had ever seen it.

"Dana, that money is for you, too," he said. "It's for you, too."

I did not want to discuss it. I was not accustomed to taking money from a man, but that was not what was making me anxious. I was unnerved by Charles's sudden desire to stock up on winter baby clothes and discuss death benefits. I could finally count the time until he came home in weeks instead of months. What was the point?

Yet as we resumed going through a stack of new sweaters and hats he had bought, I had to admit to myself that I had also been making some grim preparations. Soon after Charles arrived, I had arranged for him to meet the babysitter I had hired; I wanted him to feel comfortable with the person who would be caring for you after I returned to work. I took him to your doctor's office and pointed out how close we lived to one of the best pediatric emergency rooms in the city. As we strolled near the East River one afternoon, I showed him the mayor's mansion and told him about the high level of security in the park because of it. Without consciously thinking about it, I believe I was trying to make sure he was content with the world in which I was rearing his son—in case he never lived in it with us.

Our moods shifted from moment to moment. When Charles decided to wait until he returned for good to visit your sister and his parents, I took it as a sign that he was sure he was coming back. But as I watched him put away the baby tub and diapers, I realized that he was thinking about it differently. Charles talked to Christina often during his leave and heard from his parents and sister almost daily, but he was determined to spend the entire two weeks alone with us. They had had him for a lifetime; he knew that you might have each other for only two weeks.

Mothers being what they are, though, your grandmother King simply had to see her Chuckie. My membership in the motherhood club might have been new, but I understood completely when she called in the middle of the second week to say she would be arriving at LaGuardia Airport the following morning—just for the day. She showed up in a blue suit with a colorful silk scarf tied around her neck and her long hair twisted into a tight bun. As you know by now, Grandma King is a reserved woman who is not prone to extravagant displays of affection. So I had to laugh to myself when she smothered you with hugs and kisses even before she embraced her son.

In the taxi on the way home, I sat in the front seat and gazed in reverence at the sight of three generations of the King family together.

You got fussy that afternoon when we took your grandmother to lunch, and your father insisted on spiriting you over to the window as his mother and I ate. I tried to persuade him to spend time with your grandmother and enjoy his meal, but he would not hear of it. Standing at the window, rocking you and kissing your head, your father seemed to have all he needed, and in his arms you calmed down completely. Your grandmother and I could barely eat for watching the two of you together.

When Grandma King and your father kissed good-bye at the airport that evening, I felt that peculiar mixture of happiness and sadness that had haunted me all week. Time was running out. We had only three more days before Charles would leave for Iraq.

I wanted to spend the rest of our time alone, but we had promised to have dinner the following night with Gerald Boyd, my former boss, and his wife, Robin Stone. They had not been able to make it to the baby shower and I had not seen Gerald in months, so when we arrived at their brownstone in Harlem, I was startled to see how thin and weak he looked. Something was clearly wrong, but Robin and Gerald made clear that they wanted to keep the focus on Charles's homecoming.

We sat in the great room drinking cocktails as Robin prepared dinner. Gerald looked at Charles rocking with you on his chest and smiled a long time before he spoke.

"Man, this is what it's all about—family and shared goals," Gerald said.

When we sat down to eat, we held one another's hands in prayer. Gerald prayed for "whatever will be" according to God's will. I thought it a strange thing to say to a man who was returning to war. It was not until weeks later that Robin confided in me that her husband had been diagnosed with late-stage lung cancer, and I understood then why he had sounded such a note of resignation.

Robin and Gerald had a nine-year-old son, Zachary, who had eaten before we arrived and gone down to the basement to play. We had just finished our meal and your father was feeding me a piece of pie off his fork when we heard Zachary scream. Robin and Charles both took off for the basement, but Charles was the first to make it to the bottom of the stairs. Gerald followed as quickly as he could.

I heard Robin say, "Oh God."

Then, Charles said, "Son, what happened?" He did not wait for an answer, and Zachary was crying too hard to provide one anyway.

"I have to stop the bleeding," Charles said.

He ran up the stairs past me to the bathroom and grabbed

some towels, wetting one. I could see that his shirt was streaked with blood. "It looks like one of his teeth might be lodged in his lip but I need to stop the bleeding first to find out," he said.

He ran back down the stairs and I heard him tell Zachary that he was going to apply a lot of pressure to the towel on his face. He sent Robin for ice. At last Zachary's cries quieted and I heard Charles say that he wanted to take a look at the wound. It looked as though it might require stitches, he said.

"You'll be all right. Just hold this ice on your lip," Charles instructed as they climbed the stairs. Charles told Zachary's shaken parents to take him to the nearest emergency room, and we gathered our jackets. We were in a cab on the way home when Charles took a deep breath and gripped my leg. We rode in silence.

Later that night I was jolted out of sleep by the sound of Charles groaning. He was shaking his head from side to side, his face contorted, his breathing rapid.

I spoke his name softly, not wanting to startle him, then shook him gently.

"Wake up, baby, you're having a dream."

"There was so much blood," he said, his eyes half open.

"Where? Where was the blood?"

"Iraq," he said. "The children."

I kissed his eyelids and rocked him.

"You're safe now, Charles," I said. "You're home with me and Jordan."

He rolled on top of me and clung to my body.

"There was so much blood."

"I know, baby. I know. But you're home now."

I lay there, wide awake, until his breathing slowed and he fell back to sleep. My breasts ached from the pressure of his body, but I did not dare move.

By morning's light Charles seemed to have no memory of the dream, and I did not bring it up.

We had only a day left.

That night we took you with us on one last "date," to a Chinese restaurant, but you were squirming and crying and your father insisted on taking you outside. "You won't have a chance to eat any meals like this in peace until I come back," he said. I complained that he was spending too much time putting my needs before his. I told him I would tend to you, but he would have none of it. So I ate my food as fast as I could and asked for a carryout box for his. Then we walked slowly home, enjoying the evening air on a cloudless night.

Your father spent an hour and a half writing on the remaining empty pages in the journal, but he was constantly interrupted by phone calls from family and friends wanting to say good-bye. I remember how frustrated he was—he was trying so hard to stay focused on what he was writing. Then we stayed up talking and making love until dawn.

Charles took a shower and packed his bag, and I made chicken sandwiches for his lunch. You were still asleep as I lay on the couch in the living room watching him put on his uniform. I longed to take him back to bed once more, but we had run out of time.

"Why don't you just go AWOL and stay here with us?" I joked as he zipped his jacket.

"Now, Dana," he said, looking at me out of the corner of his eye, "you know you wouldn't want to be married to a coward."

"Oh, all right, go," I said playfully, as though this were an everyday good-bye.

He smiled as he laced his boots and put on his patrol cap. His transformation back into First Sergeant King was now complete.

I watched him go quietly to your crib and lower the safety rail.

He kissed you lightly and rubbed your back. You stirred and he smiled as he looked at you one last time. Then he removed a medal from his pocket—the army Combat Action Badge he had been awarded for running into the gun battle to pull wounded comrades to safety. Handing it to me, he said he did not need to wear it on his uniform to prove his bravery.

"Keep it for Jordan," your father said.

We stood in the doorway, my Charles and me, and kissed and held each other tight. He stroked my hair. It felt as though all the clocks had stopped.

"Now, you're going to marry me, right?" he asked.

"Yes," I said, trying to keep my voice from quavering. "I love you, and I would be honored to be your wife."

"I love you, too, Dana. You're my queen—remember that."

I shook my head but could no longer speak. He kissed me one last time.

We would run out of time on this earth and there would be no wedding, but I am certain that at that moment, declaring our love before God, I became his wife.

Thirteen

Dear Jordan,

On the flight back to Iraq, your father poured all his thoughts and feelings into a handwritten sixteen-page letter. He mailed it as soon as he landed, but I did not receive it until two weeks before he died. There are passages I am keeping to myself—some embarrassingly passionate, some to protect family members' feelings, some simply mundane—but on the whole the letter reveals too much of his exceptional spirit not to share.

Hello Ma,

I wanted to write you and tell you what a great time I had on my leave. It was absolutely great. We are truly blessed to have such a fun-loving son. He is a handful though. I hope you get some much needed rest. You were so tired. I don't want you to go to work like that.

Please tell all of your friends thank you for their hospitality and support. I enjoyed their company.

I know Jordan will soon appreciate all of his clothes and the play station. I will miss him, so you know I have to come home soon.

My sister was being a brat about me coming home,

*especially for Thanksgiving. It's not going to happen. I will be
there to see you and Jordan. I am really not interested in being
away from my family anymore. . . .*

*I will find out what my options are when I get back to Fort
Hood. We really have to pray about it. I would really like to be
with you and Jordan. I'm tired of being depressed from
leaving all the time. You think you can put up with me? . . .*

*I am being rude right now on the plane, but I have to keep
the light on to write you. I have a lot on my mind.*

*Can we start a 529 college savings plan for Jordan in New
York? Some states don't have it. We'll figure it out.*

*I will think of some goals for us, short-term and long-
term. This is the first time I did not bring my prayer book with
me when traveling. I guess I decided to give it a break.
Sometimes I don't know how long God wants me to wait for
things I ask for, how patient I need to be. So far all of my
prayers have been answered. The only thing, or one of the
things I've asked for that hasn't happened yet, is you and I
getting married. . . . I want us to be happy together. One
thing I don't want us to be is parents that argue all the time.*

*I owe you an explanation for why I did not call you for
weeks sometimes. I did what most people in my position do,
put my job before my family. I was having some issues at work
that I really needed to clear up before we deployed and
training that required a lot of my time. I was miserable and
thought about you every day. I felt that I had 104 soldiers that
needed me to be there for them to make sure they were ready.*

*I don't think you will ever understand. They look at me
like Jordan looks at you when you put him in the water. I have
to be there so they can see me, know that they are doing good,
that I am there to support them.*

I only have until March before I am finished working in this position. Though rewarding, I have made some sacrifices that I have regretted. I regret I could not make it to your doctors' appointments, or hold your hand and comfort you when Jordan was born. I was really disappointed that I had to miss that. I'm the one who missed out.

I am thankful that I was able to come before Jordan was born and help you get the room ready. Thank you, God. I don't know if Jordan will understand. I could hope that he would.

You know that I used to imagine that you would have our baby. I could see you opening the door holding a baby, but I couldn't see what the baby looked like because of the way you were holding him. So when I came home to visit it was exactly like I envisioned it. You were holding Jordan exactly the same way. He was old enough to turn his head and look at me. Isn't that amazing!

Before I got home I guess I had the wrong idea about living and being needed, until I spent time with you and Jordan. I felt that I was worth more to you, Jordan, and Christina not being here. I thought it would be better for you financially. I was wrong.

Like you, I'm pretty good at my job. I have to fight a lot of battles with my boss when I feel something is not right. He's a good sergeant major, always been there when I needed him. He was definitely a shoulder to cry on when Robbie died. He was there to help me bring him back to the base. Any time you are different you always have to prove yourself to be better than everyone else. I have worked hard to make up for my shortcomings. Being quiet is one of them, but when something has to be said I speak my mind, everyone here knows that.

I've had such a challenging and rewarding career in the army. They have even recognized me for my talent in art. That's more than I could ask for.

It takes a special kind of woman to be married to a soldier. He's always going on deployments or training, missing births, birthdays, and any special occasion you can imagine. You really have to be a self-motivated and strong-willed person. You spend a lot of time alone because he's gone. It's a tough job being a military spouse. Though we have had our differences you have always been there for me. Thank you.

I look forward to seeing what my options will be. I have no reservations about moving to be with you and Jordan. It's clear to me now what I need to do.

I know that we will be fine together. I want to be a good father and a crown to your head just as you will be my crown. . . . I trust you more than any person I have ever known.

What I have learned from being with you is that there is nothing God won't do for you and that the sky is the limit for us. Write it down, pray on it, and believe. God will do the rest.

Thank you for the great baby shower. Who would have thought of doing something like that for me? It's good to know that I've seen all of your friends and that I know you are in good hands.

Besides the passion, I have to let you know what else is on my mind. You are doing a great job of being a mommy. I am so proud of you. Daddy will be home soon to help with everything.

I love you,
Charles

Fourteen

Dear Jordan,

I remember it well. It was Thursday, October 12. Your father rarely called me at work and I had talked to him several days earlier, so I was surprised to pick up the phone at my desk in the newsroom and hear his voice. He seemed agitated. I asked what was wrong.

"Nothing, nothing," he said testily. "I just wanted to hear your voice."

Then Charles asked about his Biscuit and what it felt like to be back at work after my maternity leave. I told him that I hated to leave you with a babysitter because you couldn't yet talk: how would you let me know if something was wrong?

I had a meeting in five minutes. I decided to skip it.

Charles urged me to give myself more time to adjust to being a working mother, and I said I would try. Then I asked:

"Are you *sure* everything is all right?"

"Yes, yes."

"Okay, sweetie. I love you."

I do not recall if he said it back.

I should have reminded him that he had promised to take you on a carriage ride through Central Park for Christmas. I should have said that we had a wedding to plan. I should have asked if he wanted to try for another baby when he returned.

Yet I suspect my words would have changed nothing. It was simply not your father's way to avoid risks he required others to take.

> *No matter how high up you get always work as hard as or harder than the man next to you. If they see you pull your workload, you will level the plain and earn their respect. I hope I can earn my soldiers' respect being there for them and pulling my load. I hope that I can do the same for you, your mom, and Christina.*

No, probably nothing I could have said would have kept him from going out on that last mission.

THAT WARM OCTOBER day, you were sleeping so peacefully in your stroller and I was enjoying the sun on my face. We were on our way home from a baby boutique on Madison Avenue, where I had spent forty dollars for a pair of fleece-lined navy blue leather boots for your first winter. I laughed to myself as I walked, anticipating what your father would say about what I had paid: "Dana, *how* much? The boy can't even walk."

I would say that we had to make sure your little toes were warm in the stroller, and he would shake his head and let me have my way, as he almost always did.

That is what I was thinking when my cell phone rang as I pushed you up York Avenue.

"Where are you?" Robin asked.

"I just bought shoes for Jordan. I'm about ten minutes from home."

"I'm driving over there right now," she said.

It was not like Robin to visit uninvited but with Gerald's health steadily deteriorating, she often needed to talk.

"God, please give me the right words to comfort Robin," I prayed, as I pushed you the final few blocks home.

I was slipping your arms out of a blue jacket when the doorman buzzed and said that Robin was in the lobby. I will never forget the weariness on her face when I opened the door, the deep lines in her forehead, and the tightness of her jawline. She looked suddenly older. I worried that Gerald had taken a turn for the worse. She sighed deeply and embraced me more tightly than she ever had.

I sat her down and put you into her arms. "He'll make you feel better," I said. I thought a glass of wine might relax her and asked whether she wanted red or white.

"It doesn't matter," she said. She was in bad shape.

I had just brought a glass of Chardonnay into the living room when the phone rang.

"I don't have to answer it," I told her.

"I think you should," Robin said.

As soon as I heard Charles's mother's voice, I knew something was wrong. His sister was on the line, too. Why would they be calling together?

"Something has happened to Chuck," his mother said.

Charles and I had talked about what we would do if he were injured in combat. We were cuddling in bed when he said he might not come back the same, physically or mentally.

I was emphatic. "If, God forbid, you lose an arm or leg over there, you will come home to us, you will grieve, and you will do your rehab here. Then you will get off your butt and help me raise this baby. I will not allow you to feel sorry for yourself for too long because at least you will still be with us. No matter what shape you're in, I'll always love you and, yes, I'll still want to make love to you for the rest of our lives."

"That would take some getting used to," Charles said, stroking my stomach.

"It would be the same if I lost a breast to cancer," I told him. "No matter what, we'll always be a family."

Now, here was his mother on the phone, about to tell me he was hurt. I braced myself, mentally preparing to nurse him back to health, to make travel arrangements, to arrange a leave of absence from work. My mother would have to babysit since I would stay with Charles until I could bring him home. I wondered if he was getting enough pain medicine, wherever he was. Had he suffered a head injury, lost both legs?

"How bad is it?" I asked.

"Dana, Chuck was killed," his mother said.

I collapsed onto the hardwood floor.

I honestly did not recognize the sound that came out of my mouth. It came from deep inside, rhythmic almost, the kind of sound a wounded animal might make alone in the wilderness. I had no more control of it than I did my body. Thank God Robin was holding you, or I would have surely dropped you.

I do not know if I lay there for five minutes or fifteen. I heard you crying and saw Robin taking you out of the room. Finally, I picked up the phone and put it to my ear. I could hear Mrs. King and Gail calling my name.

They were liars, I told myself. *How dare they say that he is dead when it is simply not possible? Why would they accept what the military said without doing any "reporting"?*

Denial is a powerful cushion against such a hard fall. I was tumbling into a hole, and denial kept me from hitting the bottom so hard that I would never climb out.

I slowly got up, still shaking so hard I could barely hold the phone.

"Are you sure?" I finally said into the receiver.

"Yes, we're sure," one of them said. "The military was just here."

They can make mistakes, I wanted to yell.

"He was riding in a convoy and a roadside bomb exploded under his Humvee," one of them said. They were speaking to me as calmly and slowly as my college algebra professor used to when he explained a formula to me for the third time.

I wanted to hold my Charles, kiss his lips, wrap my arms around his body.

"Where is he?"

"He is on his way to Dover," Gail said. That was the air force base in Delaware, where the military first brings its fallen soldiers. "One of his soldiers is with him."

That's good, I thought. *He won't be alone.*

"The military is on the way to see you," Mrs. King said.

"Oh my God, what about Christina?"

"The military has already been to her house," Mrs. King said. "They notified her first. She called me crying hysterically. Her mother is with her."

Robin had come back and was bouncing you in her arms. You had stopped crying but looked frightened.

Now, how am I going to help Robin? I wondered.

But Robin had not been there because of Gerald. My mother had called her—after hearing from Mrs. King—and asked her to be with me when I received the news. Robin had known when she walked in the door that Charles was dead. She had let me pour wine and talk as if I still had my man and you still had a father. I was irrationally furious with her for an instant but then realized what an impossible situation she had been in.

At some point, I heard Robin say, "Dana, you have to pull yourself together, for Jordan."

Didn't she realize that it had taken everything inside of me just to get off the floor?

I paced for the next few hours, making phone calls to my parents, our closest friends, my office, and your babysitter. I put Charles's watch on, smelled his clothes. I was so angry that we had sent them to the laundry before he left, washing away his scent and, to my mind, his essence. I picked up a pair of his black dress shoes hoping that the socks he had left in them might still bear a trace of him. I smelled only leather.

My boss arrived with bags of barbequed ribs, mashed potatoes, and asparagus. So many neighbors and friends came to be with us until our family arrived that the doorman let them in unannounced. People took turns holding you, but you got fussy and I realized you were hungry.

I pulled you to me and nursed you. You began suckling voraciously, as if my warm milk was a tonic for your own little aching soul. You fell asleep in my arms and I wanted to follow you. My fatigue had begun to crowd out my pain.

I could hear hushed chatter coming from the living room when I left to put you in your crib. I imagined my friends asking each other how they thought I was doing, or shaking their heads in disbelief. I rubbed your back and listened to you breathing in the dark. Your father had sworn you looked just like me, but all I could see now was him.

It was well after midnight when I persuaded everyone I needed to be alone and stood in the living room listening to the silence.

You started crying and I felt the first stirrings of hope. It was as if your father was telling me that your life and your voice were preordained to replace his.

I forced myself to drink a glass of water and take a vitamin to help keep up my milk supply. The military officials never arrived, so I put on one of Charles's shirts, took the phone off the hook, turned out all the lights, and laid you next to me in bed. The rhythm of your breathing finally lulled me to sleep. My eyes soon popped back open and I stroked your head, thinking I felt a tumor. I rubbed that spot for at least fifteen minutes. Surely God would not take your father from us and then let you have brain cancer. I decided to take you for a CAT scan and some blood work, just to be sure. You stirred as I rubbed that spot, and I could almost hear Charles whispering in my ear to calm my nerves.

Honey, it's just the grief. You're anxious and tired. Go back to sleep. I'm watching over both of you.

I could feel him there, I tell you.

The sun peeked through the blinds in the morning and I opened my eyes, remarkably calm. Had it been a dream? Then I saw the bereavement flowers on the nightstand, the first of many. Charles would never again lie next to me with you between us. I would never again feel his lips on mine.

As soon as I put the phone back on the hook, it began to ring incessantly. My sister Lynnette arrived from Los Angeles. By lunchtime I had still not eaten and my friend Dorothy talked me into walking down the street to a Japanese restaurant. I sipped green tea and cried.

"I should have married him five years ago," I said, shaking my head. "I was so arrogant and immature."

Dorothy reminded me that we were a family in most every way that mattered.

I knew she was right, but I had no pictures of us kissing at an altar, no shots of a first dance. I had our memories, Dorothy reminded me. They were images that could not be contained by a picture frame.

"Do you think he wondered where I was when he died? Do you think he was scared?"

Lynnette called. There were two military representatives sitting in my living room, she said.

I had been prepared to bombard them with questions, but when I walked in the front door, the sight of those two soldiers made me queasy. Charles's death was now official.

There were introductions, handshakes. Then Master Sergeant Michael Damitio commenced with his official duty.

"The Secretary of the Army has asked me to express his deep regret that your fiancé, First Sergeant Charles Monroe King, was killed in action near Baghdad on October 14 when an improvised explosive device detonated near his armored vehicle. The Secretary extends his deepest sympathy to you and your son in your tragic loss," Sgt. Damitio said in an impassive tone.

He assured me that my soldier was wearing full body armor at the time of his death. I almost laughed out loud. It was like telling me that Charles was wearing a life vest when he drowned. Was I meant to imagine that the armor had stopped the blast from causing his chest cavity to cave in or his skull to fracture? If I had been there as a reporter, interviewing him about someone else, I would have asked: "What exactly did all of that gear protect?" And: "Has a grieving mother or spouse ever thought that hearing about body armor made their loved one less dead?"

At the same time I felt sorry for Sgt. Damitio. He probably wished he were anywhere other than in my living room. He went on to say something about honor and heroism, but once I realized he was working from talking points, I tuned him out.

"Did he suffer?" I asked, finally.

"Ma'am, I don't know."

"Was he conscious when they pulled him out of the vehicle?"

"Again, I don't know."

"Can I show you some pictures of him?"

"Sure."

He and his silent partner nodded approvingly as I showed them photographs of your father holding you for the first time. I did not care that they were only doing their duty. I needed to talk about my Charles to anyone who would indulge me.

I said he was an artist, was so proud of his beautiful daughter and his new son, that he was coming home and retiring to marry me and to watch you grow up. They nodded some more, smiled at the appropriate times, and waited.

I stopped talking because I was about to break down, and Sgt. Damitio saw his chance. "Ma'am, we need a few pieces of information from you," he said, so quietly I almost could not hear him. "We need your son's social security number and a copy of his birth certificate."

So that was it. They were in my home to gather information, not to give it. I imagined that in death notification training they were taught not to ask for the documents too soon.

I was grateful that the corrected birth certificate with your father's name where it always should have been had arrived two days earlier. I roughly calculated the time difference between New York and Baghdad and realized it had probably come about the time he was dying. I never had the chance to tell him we had received it.

I handed Sgt. Damitio the documents he requested, said I

knew he had a difficult job, and thanked him and his partner—
who had not said a word but looked suitably solemn—for coming.
They were kind enough, but I wanted them out of my home before
I started screaming.

I closed the door behind them and sat stunned. I thought
about the sergeant's perfectly polished patent-leather shoes, his
precision haircut, and his crisp uniform. No wonder Charles had
not allowed me to do our ironing. Who could get clothes that
wrinkle-free?

Something about the formality of the sergeant's uniform, the
erectness of his back as he spoke, his robotic delivery, had left me
feeling cheated. Had he even noticed the grin on Charles's face in
those photographs of him holding you? The only evidence of emotion was the odor of cigarette smoke I thought I detected, which
told me he might have tried to calm his nerves before he arrived. I
thought about why I cared so much about this stranger's demeanor. It was, I concluded, because Sgt. Damitio represented the
entire military and government to me and so I needed him to be
personally connected to my soldier.

Did he know more than he was saying about how Charles died?
I hoped I was done dealing with military personnel and bureaucracy. In fact, it was only the beginning.

A few days later, Sgt. Damitio and his silent driver picked us up
and drove us to Fort Hamilton, in Brooklyn. The army needed to
brief me about the benefits you were entitled to receive as
Charles's dependent. They also said you needed a new military
identification card. I was not sure why.

We sat in an office while a woman pecked your information into
a computer and took your picture for the card. I looked at it and
could not tell the difference between it and the one I had gotten for
you just three months earlier. Then I saw it. The box denoting the

sponsoring soldier's military status had been changed. Instead of "active duty," it said "DEC"—deceased. I felt my stomach churn.

Soon we were shuttled into another office belonging to a rotund man with piercing eyes and a demeanor that made Sgt. Damitio seem downright effusive. He gave me his card, which said "Retirement Services Officer." I sat there holding you tightly as the man talked about survivor benefits and one-time emergency grants that help families in my situation keep the lights on during financial hardships. Then he said I might have trouble obtaining all that we were entitled to because I'd had you "out of wedlock."

I had no energy to challenge him. Instead, I sighed, and tears ran down my face.

"My sweet, sweet Charles, how did we end up here?" I thought to myself.

Then the officer said something that snapped me back to attention: "All right, I know you're nervous, but you need to calm down."

It was the second insult in a matter of minutes. First he had treated me like some bimbo with a baby in tow who had come calling for her dead man's money. Then he had the audacity to tell me how to express my grief. I had not so much as whimpered as I sat there, but even if I had, that man had no right to tell me to calm down. I was furious. My head felt like it was going to explode from the anger surging through me.

I stood up and looked into his eyes to let him know I was not intimidated. "First of all, I am not nervous," I said. "I am hurting. Charles may just be a number in a file to you, but he was the man I loved and the father of my child. We planned this baby and you have no right to judge."

I pulled a picture out of my purse of your father and me boarding a cruise ship and shoved it in the man's direction.

"Look at this," I insisted, "so that you'll remember the next time someone like me is sitting in front of you that their loved one was a person."

I turned to Sgt. Damitio. "He's a jerk, and I'm not sitting here any longer," I said and walked out of the building and into the sunlight with you in my arms. I knew I had violated some sort of military protocol, but I was not going to sit there and let that bureaucrat offend me. I knew Charles would have expected no less of me.

When we got home, the message light on my answering machine was blinking. Among the dozens of messages from family, friends, and colleagues was an unfamiliar voice: a man who sounded raspy and far away—and anguished.

"This is First Sergeant Wesley," he said. "I'm calling from Iraq. I was a friend of First Sergeant King's and we loved him very much. I know you are already aware of what happened. First Sergeant King gave me your number and he asked me to contact you to make sure you were all right if anything ever happened to him. I'll call again to check on you when I return to the states in a few weeks."

I felt a surge of energy. Not even death could keep Charles from finding a way to let me know he was protecting us. For that moment, anyway, I could feel his embrace.

Sgt. Wesley never did call again, but his message had served its purpose. I played it over and over when I was at my lowest.

Cesar, the doorman of my building, stopped by one afternoon, hat over his heart, with a story to tell. That last morning, he told me, Charles was plainly crying when he emerged from the elevator. He motioned for Cesar to come near.

"How can I leave my family? I need more time," Charles said softly. "Please look out for them."

Cesar hugged your dad and promised that he would. Before he could say more, Charles said he could not stay any longer. He picked up his duffle bag and was gone.

Hearing this story, I wept. The Charles who had kissed me good-bye had been strong and unflinching. He had protected me from his tears, perhaps knowing that if he showed them to me, I would have done anything in my power to keep him with me.

A few days later, the phone rang and another unfamiliar voice asked for me. It was Charles's ex-wife, Cecilia. I had talked to Christina the day after we learned of your father's death, but I had never expected to speak to her mother.

"Dana, I just wanted to call and say I am so sorry," Cecilia said. "I've been thinking about what to say to comfort you. Chuck loved you and Jordan very much. I want to say that I've had a chance to watch Christina grow up with some of the same qualities as her father. You have that to look forward to in Jordan."

I started sobbing.

"Cecilia, thank you so much," I cried. "I know you're hurting, too. I just don't know what to say."

She said that she was holding up and trying to be strong for Christina. She said I should call if there was anything at all she could do. I will never forget her graciousness, and the way it momentarily eased my suffering.

Every part of me ached for Charles, but anger at him for having left us was beginning to creep in. Your father and I had been having a playful argument just before he returned to Iraq about what kind of dog to get for you someday. Charles wanted a Great Dane or a German Shepherd. I wanted a "teacup" dog.

"Not no oversized rat," he protested.

"All right," I said, "but if you go and die on me, you will lose this argument. I will get a dog so tiny I can carry it in my purse."

Now I was without him and all I wanted was another chance to bicker about dogs or how much I had spent on your shoes or how we planned to discipline you in the years ahead. (Charles was more of a strict disciplinarian.) I wanted to punch him for leaving me. I wanted to go to bed, pull the covers over my head, and stay there forever.

But in you, Charles had given me a precious gift, and you deserved something more. A strong mother. Even a strong overwrought mother.

Still, as I thought about the future that morning, I could not see very far—only as far as his funeral and the long, harsh winter so suddenly upon us.

Fifteen

Dear Jordan,

It's time I told you how your father died. This has been the most painful thing I have ever written, and it will likely be the most difficult thing you will ever read. But I believe I owe you the most precise account I can provide of that dreadful day.

It must surely have been God's design that Charles fell in love with a journalist, for in order to reconstruct your father's final day, I have drawn on all the skills I learned in nearly twenty years of reporting. Never did I think they would be put to such use. Sometimes I cried myself to sleep after interviewing people who provided graphic details of the scene. As wrenching as the work was, though, I could not let go until I knew the truth.

I began by talking to nearly a dozen of your father's soldiers, often in late-night phone calls when they were off work and you were asleep. I interviewed men who were with your father on his last convoy and the medic who treated him at the scene. I spoke to his company, battalion, and brigade commanders, to his "battle buddy," and to the wife of a soldier who died with him. I also spoke to the doctor who was on duty at the hospital in Baghdad when Charles arrived the day he died and to the officer who formally identified his body and watched as a chaplain administered Last Rites. I pored over sworn statements from soldiers who were in the vicinity of the blast that day, commanders' memorandums, and summaries of battalion operations reports. I steeped myself in army literature on fighting insurgents and guarding against IEDs. I also conducted more than a dozen interviews with a spokesman for army personnel who works at the Pentagon, Major Nathan Banks. He reviewed your father's case and was able to fill in crucial details, verify information, and give me a larger picture of how the military operates and what happened the day your father died. Here is what I can tell you:

On Saturday, October 14, 2006, at 0946 hours Baghdad time, your father and his six-vehicle convoy rolled out of the forward operating base, traveling south before crossing the Euphrates River and turning north on Route Patty toward the Island. They were on a routine supply mission, delivering food, water, ammunition, batteries, and other necessities to about sixty of his troops who had been conducting surveillances and raids from the Island. The convoy included a forward and rear tank, two mobile infantry carriers outfitted with weapons, one Humvee, and a supply truck capable of carrying five tons of rations.

At 1038 hours, the convoy passed through the town of Jurf as-Sakhr, where Iraqis were doing their morning shopping. A few of the soldiers noticed a date shop that seemed open but strangely empty of merchants and customers, but no one was troubled enough to halt the formation. The convoy was about two miles from the Island, just past that date shop, when insurgents detonated a large IED, using a trip wire that ran through the trees. The IED ripped through the bottom of a vehicle in the middle of the formation, the Humvee, which burst into flames. One soldier, Sergeant William Record, was critically burned on his face and arms. Specialist Timothy Lauer, Staff Sergeant Joseph Kane, and First Sergeant Charles King were killed. On the official reports, your father was pronounced dead at 1039 hours.

These are the bare facts, at least according to the military, but over the past year I have learned so much more.

Not long after the explosion that killed your father, a sniper team that had just arrived noticed two civilian men fleeing in the direction of a nearby shack, but the suspects escaped. Then, suddenly, a white minivan was driving toward them and ignoring hand and arm signals and warnings shouted in both Arabic and English for the driver to halt. The snipers fired a warning shot into the air and then several shots into the van's engine block, but the vehicle continued forward. They sprayed it with rounds from their M14 rifles until it stopped. When two men attempted to flee the vehicle, the snipers shot and killed them. They then noticed more passengers, including a man alternately peeking over the dashboard and ducking beneath it. The soldiers fired additional rounds into the vehicle. When they finally approached, they found that man and four women inside. There were no weapons or explosives.

One of the women was five months pregnant; she was alive but had been shot in the abdomen. The soldiers immediately sought medical help, but I have not been able to determine her fate. The thought of her baby dying from a gunshot wound before he or she ever took a breath haunts me. The child would now be about a year old.

Some of your father's comrades consoled themselves in the days after he died by spreading word that "we got 'em." During a memorial service the Dealers held in Iraq, Lt. Col. Patrick Donahoe, the battalion commander, told his men that, while the enemy had struck a despicable blow, "we must remember that on the fourteenth, not only our men died, but we shot and killed the two we know to be responsible."

I asked Donahoe recently how he could have been sure. His answer was unsettling.

"I am not really sure, to be honest," he said. "We did engage a car that day and a couple of folks were killed there. I think we want to believe that they were involved, but we had no real, hard direct evidence."

The men and their passengers in that van may well have been insurgents fleeing with their families, or they might simply have been confused civilians who panicked when they came upon the Americans.

What Donahoe did not say is that the killings were convenient on a number of levels. They provided closure, militarily. And they gave the Dealers, especially the Carnivores, a place to direct their anger.

A military inquest found that the snipers were justified in taking the actions they did. I do not disagree with that conclusion. The snipers, as far as I can tell, did not kill those people out of revenge, and had given the Iraqis several opportunities to stop and get out of their van before firing upon it.

What I am not so comfortable with is celebrating those deaths as vindication for your father's.

About two weeks after Charles's death, I received a letter of condolence from Donahoe, who wrote: "The powerful explosive ripped through the bottom of the vehicle he was riding in, killing him, we believe, immediately. . . . We now go forward from this place on the Euphrates River with heavy hearts. We press on with the mission here."

The army's formal position, made clear in the letter, was that Charles had died instantly. At the time I accepted it. Most people, I assume, accept the military's official account of their soldier's death. But as I learned, the military often sanitizes the truth. And saying a soldier died instantly when the facts tell another story is only the beginning of the official spin.

In a little-known office in Aberdeen Proving Ground,

Maryland, more than two dozen military employees and civilian contract workers go through every item of a dead soldier's belongings, looking for anything sensitive or scandalous. The workers read the soldiers' letters and e-mail messages. They listen to their music and watch their DVDs. They review the contents of their cameras and video recorders. They literally go through soldiers' dirty laundry.

The scrubbing, as the examination is called, is primarily done to identify and confiscate classified information or sensitive material in a soldier's possession. If the scrubbers do their jobs properly, families will never see photographs of dead or bloodied prisoners, or maps pinpointing secret military facilities.

But there is another reason for it.

The military regards sanitizing a soldier's belongings as a last act of protecting one of its own. So, in consultation with a soldier's battle buddies, military representatives take it upon themselves to change the story those items sometimes tell. They will tear a suicide note out of a soldier's diary. They will destroy sexually explicit letters from a girlfriend so that a wife never sees them. They will clean blood off clothing before returning it to a father. They will send a mangled wedding band to a jeweler in order to return it to a grieving spouse in pristine condition.

These facts, disclosed to me by a high-ranking military official who believes in this system, turned my world upside down. I trusted Charles and had no desire to see his dirty laundry, in any sense. But now I was determined to find out the truth about his death.

In the official version, he did not survive the blast, had never felt the excruciating pain of his bones crumbling like crackers. In my mind, Charles had gone from an earthly world to a heavenly one with little or no transition. I could accept that. But after talking to his troops, I no longer believe that is what happened.

I interviewed Corporal Jason Imhoff several times, beginning about six months after Charlie Company returned to Fort Hood. His account of that day was radically different. When the convoy departed from the FOB that morning, Imhoff was the gunner on the lead tank, tasked with spotting IEDs.

"Me and my tank commander got pretty good at finding roadside bombs before they killed anyone," Imhoff told me. "My main job was to look through my sights and keep scanning to make sure everything was in order."

He then interrupted his account. "I still feel like it's personally my fault," he said. "I feel like I let him down."

But there were extenuating circumstances. There had been a rainstorm early that morning and the wet road concealed the fresh dirt that had been packed over the hole in which the bomb was hidden. The triggerman was well out of sight: several soldiers followed the wire that was used to detonate the explosive to his position on a dirt mound in a nearby canal.

In any case, I assured Imhoff that Charles would not want him to blame himself for not detecting the IED. My words did not have much effect. But he went on.

"I was scanning the road and we were almost at the Island. Then our tank commander started saying, 'IED, IED.'"

Soldiers and civilians for miles around recognized the all-too-familiar boom. Like a period at the end of a sentence, it was a sound that stopped all conversation. Except at the scene.

"We started firing machine guns. There were lots of weeds in the area where bad guys could hide," Imhoff said. "It was very chaotic on the radios. They were sending information about who was hurt. I tried to talk to the tank in the rear and they said they were going to pick up casualties and take them to the landing zone for the MEDEVAC."

Word eventually came that Charles's vehicle was the one that had been hit.

"They finally gave his battle roster number, which is a sequence of letters and numbers, and we knew who it was," Imhoff said. "I cried."

The attack was one of the worst the soldiers had seen. Back at the FOB, Charles's roommate Tony noticed the commotion. Someone told him Charlie Company had been hit. Was Top King on the convoy? he asked. No one would answer, so he rushed to the scene in search of his friend. He could not believe what he saw.

"Let me tell you, when I seen that Humvee, I knew," Tony said.

The explosive had detonated under the middle of the vehicle, sending it six to eight feet in the air and blowing off the doors as well as the massive gun turret, which is the size of a small Volkswagen and movable only by crane. The blast created a crater that was six feet deep by ten feet wide. It ejected all four occupants.

It was likely by design that the insurgents had detonated the bomb at the center of the formation. They had been in battle with the Americans long enough to know that the senior officer never rides in back, which in U.S. military culture would be tantamount to trailing soldiers—like a coward—in combat. They knew, too, that the leader's vehicle is typically in the middle of a convoy. That position provides the best "situational awareness" of the battlefield—the optimal view of what is happening in front of and behind the ranking soldier.

"I don't know if anyone has told you this," Imhoff said, then paused as if waiting for a sign from me to continue. I told him to go on. "After the explosion, he was alive and he was talking."

He said Charles was in shock and grunting, but that even as he lay dying he was thinking of his men. "He asked about the other soldiers," Imhoff said.

I tried unsuccessfully to swat away a selfish thought. "Do you think he thought about us, too?" I asked the corporal. It was not a reporter's question, of course. It had no answer. It was a widow's inquiry, and it was unfair of me to ask.

Imhoff assured me that, if it were at all possible to have such thoughts at a moment like that, my soldier surely did. What else was he to say?

If Imhoff was correct, not only had Charles been alive after he was struck, he had been able to speak. If he could speak, he could feel. He might have felt the pain of his organs having ruptured. He might have struggled to breathe. He might have wondered in his delirium why I was not there with him. In any case, it was not the mercifully swift death I had imagined.

I paced our apartment and tried to process what Imhoff had said. I sobbed. I had nightmares for weeks, in which I and the people I loved were under attack. Bullets whizzed past my head. One time I was on a plane being shot down by terrorists. Each time I awoke from one of these dreams, I bolted upright, breathing rapidly and sometimes clutching my chest. But I had to continue with my reporting.

As you slept one winter night in early 2007, I called Sgt. Adam Martínez, who was in the last tank in the convoy that day. He was the first person to reach Charles at the scene.

"I saw the Humvee doing a 360, like spinning around in flames," Martínez told me. "I saw the driver, Sergeant Record, sitting on the ground burning and screaming in flames." (Despite severe burns, Record survived.)

"First Sergeant King was already out of the Humvee, standing straight up in the middle of the road," Martínez said. Charles stood for about thirty seconds, according to Martínez, then fell forward and landed facedown.

"I ran to the Humvee first. I wanted to make sure no one was in there burning. Then I ran back around and said 'First Sergeant, can you hear me?'" He said Charles groaned. Martínez asked again if Charles could hear him and told him to grunt if he understood. Charles groaned again.

"Rounds were popping off and I was trying to get him out of there and he wouldn't move. At that point I grabbed him and pulled as hard as I could. I guess what you call the adrenaline kicked in. I kept dragging and pulling him until we got to a ditch that had better cover and concealment for us."

Charles looked him in the eyes, Martínez said. My heart hurt as he spoke.

"I noticed bleeding from his mouth and nose, and the corners of his eyes were bloodshot. So I started first aid, but there was nothing I could really do for him. He took a deep breath and sighed. Doc got there at that time and took over. I got back in my tank because I needed to pull up to cover the guys from the rounds cooking off and shooting over our heads."

Martínez had broken protocol and disregarded what Charles had taught him about not entering a "kill zone" until it was safe to do so. It was Martínez, in fact, who helped me to understand how soldiers could set aside their instincts for self-preservation to save a comrade—as thousands of them, men and women, are doing without acclaim in Iraq and Afghanistan, even as I type these words.

"It's something you don't think about," he said of his actions the day he rushed into danger to tend to my Charles. "I wasn't going to leave our guys out there."

I was not sure I could listen to any more tales of how my man had died, but there was one more person I needed to talk to: Specialist Harold "Doc" García, the medic who had treated Charles after the explosion.

Doc had been in the second vehicle in your father's convoy

that day. By the time he reached Charles, he told me, he could not find a heartbeat. "There was nothing, no pulse," Doc said. "Bullets were flying and I was like 'shit, man,' you know?" Despite the danger from the gunfire, and the likelihood that Charles had already died, Doc administered CPR.

"I gave him a breath and went and gave him compressions, but as soon as I pressed down I could tell his chest cavity was kind of crushed. I knew he'd passed away," he said.

Like Martínez, however, Doc broke protocol because he was not ready to give up on saving his Top.

"After we knew he passed away we actually treated him like there was hope because we couldn't believe it," Doc said. The men put him on a stretcher and put an IV line in his arm, he told me.

"We were going down the road with him on top of the tank and it was unbelievable what we did. You never ride outside because of the threat of another bomb. We just wanted to get him to the bird," he said, referring to the MEDEVAC helicopter, "so we pulled some crazy stuff like that."

Doc said Charles would have done the same for any of them. "He would never leave nobody," he said. "I know first sergeants that would never lead the missions, would never leave the FOB. He was the best damn first sergeant I've ever seen."

The men of Charlie Company were devastated by Charles's death, none more than Sergeant Shoan Mohammed. "I was supposed to go on the convoy First Sergeant King went on," he told me. "That was supposed to be me in that vehicle."

Charles had told Mohammed that he could remain at the base to take care of paperwork.

"I didn't believe it was true," Mohammed said quietly. "First Sergeant King was a big man and a strong man. Nobody ever thought any harm would ever come to him. He was the rock of our company. You can't replace someone like the first sergeant. We didn't know how to exactly cope."

Mohammed told me that even some of the officers fell to their knees and wept in the hours after Charles died. Other soldiers could not eat or sleep.

"I think we were silent for a few days before we could really speak about it," Mohammed said. "Then the commander pulled us together. We had our ceremony as we did for the other comrades who had fallen. As we did our salutes and tribute to him it finally started sinking in, but what helped us most was when we did our prayer vigil for First Sergeant King and expressed what he meant to us."

It was unusual for Captain McFarland to lead a prayer vigil, but he had no choice. The person to whom he had always delegated that task, Charles, was no longer among them.

Three of his men had told me that Charles had survived the initial blast. Now I called Dr. Steven Taylor, an army major who was on duty at a hospital in Baghdad the day your father died. Perhaps he could tell me whether Charles had been alive when his men brought him in. Taylor's response was chilling. "Ma'am, I'm sorry. I honestly don't remember him." Taylor explained that he worked in the largest combat support hospital in Iraq, and that he and two other doctors had treated about fifteen thousand American soldiers during their yearlong tour of duty. Nothing about my soldier stood out.

Not remember my Charles? I could not imagine it, just as I still did not know why a soldier as senior as a first sergeant had been out on a resupply mission in the first place. This is where Charlie Company's culture gets complicated. Mohammed thinks Charles had an unusual view of his responsibilities, which I believe McFarland strongly encouraged.

"A first sergeant's job is not to go out there and go up and down on dangerous routes every day," said Mohammed. "It doesn't require you to go outside the compound of safety as much. But First Sergeant King was not only willing, he went outside the compound every day."

I asked a military official with command experience for his view. Was Charles's determination commendable or reckless? Would an officer with more experience than McFarland have used his first sergeant more strategically?

The official was dismayed. He likened the approach to sending a pilot out of the cockpit to serve drinks. "You have your Top out there in the red zone and you're encouraging it?" the officer said, incredulous. "If you're a commander, that's your lifeline, and you've got him out there playing in traffic."

Was he suggesting that the value of a soldier's life was somehow related to his rank?

Yes, he said. He was speaking of losses in terms of military needs, not personal suffering. That was the harsh reality of war.

"Forgive me if it sounds cruel, but we can get another soldier to replace the driver," the officer said. "But we can't replace your leadership. That takes years and experience to build. When you take down a first sergeant, you leave a big void in the operation. It's a big kill. A first sergeant leads everyone. They took nineteen years of experience away from us that day."

Charles had promised me, when we parted last, that he wouldn't take unnecessary chances. Was there something I did not know? Some specific reason for going out that day?

Charles's battle buddy, Tony, had noticed that Charles was morose the week he died.

"It started Tuesday or Wednesday night," Tony told me. "I was like 'King, what's wrong, man?' He said 'Man, my commander pissed me off.' King heard that his commander had called people back on the FOB 'FOBettes,' meaning you didn't bust the wire or go outside the gate."

He might just as well have called them majorettes or cheer-leaders—sissies. Charles told Tony that McFarland had taunted him. "Are you coming off the wire or are you going to stay back with all the other FOBettes?" he said his commander had asked.

Tony tried to bolster Charles's spirits over the next two days. He also reminded him of their agreement: "When we returned from leave we had made a pact that we didn't need to go outside the gate anymore," Tony said. "We had a lot of things to do on the in-side to prepare the soldiers for redeployment back to the continen-tal United States. That was our mission.

"I said, 'To hell with that guy, man. You don't need to go out that wire. We already talked about it, King. You've been out that wire more than anyone around here.' But it weighed heavily on his mind. And he talked about going out again on Friday."

Tony reiterated that Charles had nothing to prove. He offered to accompany him on the mission planned for the following morn-ing if Charles still insisted on going.

"He just said, 'All right,'" Tony recalled.

I believe that by going on that final mission Charles was not only trying to earn his soldiers' respect, but also to impress his commander one more time. Before he retired, he wanted to be promoted to sergeant major, the highest rank an enlisted soldier can attain. It was Captain McFarland who would evaluate him for the position.

I am convinced that Charles had made up his mind to join the convoy by the time he placed the call to my office a few days earlier, and certainly by the time Tony made a final plea to him to stay be-hind. Sometime in the predawn hours that followed their last conversation, only one month short of the end of his tour, Charles slipped quietly out of his room, careful not to wake his roommate.

"I didn't hear nothing from him that morning," Tony said. "That wasn't like him. He'd usually say, 'I'm going here,' and I'd say, 'Let me get my stuff and I'll roll with you.'"

Tony said that Charles knew he would not have let him break the pact without a fight. "I would have gone with him and he would not have wanted me out there," Tony said. "Or if he had told me he was going, he knew I would have stopped him."

No one could stop Charles, though. This was a solitary mission to defend his honor. It is clear from his journal that Charles would do whatever he thought he had to do to preserve his dignity.

> *Son, for the life of me I can't figure it out, but some people will always take an opportunity to make you feel less or incapable. Sometimes you have to be a fierce warrior, but commitment to anything will earn you anybody's respect. And adversity will make you stronger if you let or allow it to. Don't get angry with your adversaries; get even by proving them wrong. Loud, emotional people waste a lot of energy.*

By order of Colonel John Tully, brigade commander, Route Patty and the Island were abandoned within days of your father's death. The road had been an issue for months, I discovered. Tully's superior, division commander General James Thurman, did not think the army had adequate route-clearing equipment to make Route Patty safe for soldiers to travel to the Island. But the general had deferred to his officers.

"The decision to close the Island patrol base was a decision that I made after Charles and Kane and Lauer died," Tully said. "I just reached a point in my mind where the cost was just outweighing the benefits of being out on that patrol base."

If only he had acted sooner. If only McFarland—and Charles—had not argued for months prior in favor of keeping the Island operating despite the dangers.

General Thurman flew to Cleveland from Washington to attend your father's funeral and shook my hand after the service. He patted your back and said he was sorry for our loss. I believed him and appreciated him being there. I still do, even though he declined months later through a spokesman to talk to me. He also declined to respond to written questions I offered to submit about why the army had ever used the Island and similar small, isolated bases that left the soldiers largely unprotected.

I also had questions for Captain McFarland, but it took me the better part of a year to find the strength to phone him. I was afraid of what he might say, and of what I might say to him. When I finally made the call, in the winter of 2007, my hands were shaking.

By then he had a desk job: assistant professor of military science at the University of Texas. He was still on active duty, but as an instructor, he was ineligible for redeployment. He said he had put off calling me, too. So we had that in common.

The conversation was awkward. To me, he had come to stand for the military itself, for an impersonal system that had stolen the father of my child. But I was afraid that if he knew how bitter I felt toward him, he would not open up. So I interviewed him with the same dispassionate demeanor I had shown as a cub reporter on the police beat when an officer initiated me by making me interview him with a dead body lying at our feet.

I asked McFarland how he understood the job of first sergeant.

"It's where the rubber meets the road at the company level," he told me. "He's the top dog. He enforces all the standards, he's the disciplinarian, he's the subject matter expert. He makes sure the soldiers get fed, that they get their bullets, that they've been trained."

He said that Charles had been unlike any other first sergeant he had ever seen. "We were both fighters," he said. "That's why we both had such good reputations in the company. He used to go load on the tank. We had guys who had gone on leave and if we were shorthanded he'd get out there and help. That's why he left the FOB that day. The soldiers had been out there, slugging it out, for two weeks. He wanted to make sure they had hot food for the first time in a few days and all the fuel and bullets they needed."

I wanted to know if he thought, in retrospect, that Charles had stepped outside the traditional role of first sergeant.

"Being the kind of leader he was, he felt like it was his responsibility, and I felt rightly so," McFarland said. "Other first sergeants spent one-tenth of the time outside the wire. He gave everything, and people said that before this ever happened."

What was the relationship between a commander and a first sergeant? I asked.

"Like husband and wife."

Had there been tension between them?

"We worked so well hand-in-hand together," he said. "We had our differences. So many nights we stayed in the office and talked, figuring out what was going right and what was going wrong. He and I were very alike. When we were at work, we were fully committed to work. I've got two kids and a third on the way, but when I walked into the office in the morning, I had 109 children to take care of, love, and nurture, and they were in a heck of a lot worse situation than our kids back home. But whenever I walked in the door at home—and he was the same way—my full priority was my family."

Instinct told me that McFarland was not a man prone to displays of emotion, but he became more emotional as we talked. He told me that he and his wife were expecting a son and that they planned to name him Charles. I was touched and jealous. I couldn't help but think that Charles and I would never have another baby of our own.

"He was one of the greatest men I have ever known," the captain said. "He gave everything. I love that man. Oh, I had the ultimate man-love for that man. That's the biggest compliment I could give him."

I am not going to write everything that McFarland told me about the scene of the explosion because some of it is simply too gruesome. At times, he was unbearably frank, as though he were unburdening himself, as though he had forgotten that Charles had been my fiancé.

"My first impression was holy crap, I'd never seen a Humvee that damaged before," McFarland said. "I talked to Doc, our medic. Doc ran up to Top and tried to do chest compressions and saw blood coming out of his ears, mouth, and all of his extremities. The concussion had killed him instantly."

I asked what he made of the conflicting reports about Charles being conscious and speaking after the blast. He offered a grim theory.

"The only thing I can imagine is that his eyes were open, so people probably thought that he was alive. And they probably thought it was a nice thing to say that he asked about his soldiers. In any of these situations you have three or four different stories.

"He died a soldier's death and I will take that any day over rotting from cancer or anything else. He died a glorious soldier's death out doing great things for God and country. Jordan has got to be so proud and just live that pride."

I wanted to scream at him to look you in the eye, Jordan, and speak those words about your father's "glorious" death. I needed him to keep talking, though, so I said nothing. In fact, I waited more than an hour to ask about what mattered most to me. As a reporter I knew it was often best to save your toughest question for last, when you have gained your subject's trust.

"Now I'm going to ask you something difficult," I said, my voice calm but my whole body tense. "I've been told that there was some tension between you and Charles, and that he might have gone out on that mission because you taunted him. I was told that you called him a FOBette. I just want to know what you can tell me about that."

His answer was swift. "No, I didn't say that. I would never have called him a FOBette. I had too much respect for him to do that."

"All right, if you say it's not true, that's good enough for me," I said.

I was not sure I meant it, but I felt sorry for McFarland. He was grieving for Charles, too.

We had begun to talk about something else when the captain interrupted me.

"Well, wait a minute," McFarland said. "Honestly, as I think about it, there is probably some truth to that. I don't remember that discussion, but that's entirely possible, it really is. He may have started to feel as if I was wondering where he was at. That's entirely possible. I have to think about that for a while. A lot of people at the end didn't want to go out. There was light at the end of the tunnel, and the light was very bright."

I did not sleep for days after that. Images of Charles's death flooded my mind. Over and over I heard McFarland admitting it was "possible" that he had said something that had goaded Charles into going back outside of the wire.

In time I would come to see that my resentment was misplaced. What I was most angry about was that you would never have a father and that I would never again have my wonderful man. That was ultimately neither McFarland's nor Charles's fault—although there are days when I am still gripped with anger toward them.

Perhaps it was my grief that had made me second-guess the decisions your father and his commander made. I wondered whether I would have had the same questions if I were reporting about any other first sergeant who had died in similar circumstances. As a civilian with no experience in war, did I even have the right to question the decisions they made?

Perhaps under the pressure of war, what begins as a kind of machismo ribbing becomes more serious and, in your father's case, prompted him to join the doomed convoy. In any case, Charles, who had served four combat tours, who had received more than fifty commendations for his dedication and bravery, who had missed your birth because of his devotion to duty, set out to prove himself one last time.

I do not believe McFarland's claim that Charles died instantly, but he was truthful when he said that in these circumstances there are usually "three or four different stories." In the case of your father's death, not all the discrepancies are lies. Soldiers who arrived at the scene after he had been evacuated recounted secondhand information. Others sought to bolster their beloved Top's heroism. And some of the men did a kind of scrubbing of their own, not wanting to add to my grief by disclosing grim details of the carnage.

Digging down to the truth of a story is what I do. This was no different. Here is what I now believe about how my soldier—your father—died:

I believe Charles was alive after the bomb exploded that October day, and that he may have lived for ten to twenty minutes after the blast, bleeding internally. I believe he tried to speak but could not. I believe he was in shock and did not suffer much. I believe those angel wings he drew carried his spirit to a place with no bombs and no unfriendly borders.

Sixteen

Dear Jordan,

I am not sure whether I am more grateful that you were too young to remember the day we buried your father or sorry that you did not have the chance to say good-bye.

We flew to Cleveland on a gray, chilly afternoon in October. As the plane descended, I watched the landscape come into view. The dogwoods and apple trees still held on to their gold, yellow, and rust leaves—yet all I could think was that the branches would soon be bare.

I held tight to you as we landed: you were my protector, my reminder that life, even at its cruelest, is a miracle. I would hold you that way for most of the two days ahead.

When we arrived at our hotel, your grandmothers gently coaxed me into letting go of you long enough for me to spend time alone at the funeral home with my Charles. He would not have wanted you there, I knew.

I walked slowly into the large parlor where his cold, steel casket sat closed under an American flag. The staff had tried to warm the room with soft music, low lighting, and bright floral arrangements, but still I shivered. I placed my hand on the steel where I imagined his head and chest rested, patted those places, and then lay my head down on them. It was the last time we would be alone. I briefly thought of asking the funeral director to open the casket so I could kiss his face, but I knew it would be cold and stiff, nothing like my Charles.

I sat with him a long while, told him that I loved him, that you were doing fine, that I was holding up as well as I could without my best friend. I considered staying all night next to him, but I knew he would not want me to spend my first night away from you in a funeral home. So I stood up and talked to him one last time.

> *Sweetie, I want you to rest now. Your work here is done: let me finish what we started.*
>
> *I want to thank you for our son. I will raise him to be the kind of man you were. The journal will help me, and I am so grateful for that.*
>
> *I will be okay, in time, but I don't want you to think that means that I'll ever stop loving you. I never will. And I promise that Jordan will know you. You will never be replaced.*
>
> *Thank you for showing me what real love looks like and feels like. You rest now, baby. I love you.*

I kissed the casket lightly and let my tears fall on it.

The funeral director was outside, and I asked him to put a package inside the casket: a blue and white pacifier that said "I love daddy"; a camouflage-patterned onesie you had worn; a photo of the three of us smiling with a note from me to Charles on the back.

"I'll place it next to his heart," the man said.

The thought of that made me smile, but the reporter in me wondered how many times this man in the grief business had made that same promise to a mourning mother or lover. I told myself that Charles's heart was with me now, not in that box. Still, it gave me solace to think of the package resting on his chest, which I suppose was the point.

One more month, I thought. He would have been home in one more month.

Mourners were arriving at our hotel from all over the country, and as we received them in a banquet room, I knew that Charles would have loved introducing his son to so many friends and relatives. Another of the many things he would never do with you. Just the hope of watching you struggle with wrapping paper on your first Christmas had kept him going as those bombs were exploding around him.

> *[My biggest fear is] not being around to watch you and Christina grow up. At least watching you learn how to walk. My greatest joy at this time in my life is knowing that you will be born.*

I needed to hold you again to steady myself as we sat there with so many people kissing and rubbing your head. You were tired, I could see, but not fussy, in your blue sweater and tan pants. I knew why they longed to touch you, but I gave up any pretense of politeness and forcefully said no when anyone asked to hold you. As long as you were safe in my arms, a piece of your father was as well.

I spent the next hour talking about your cesarean birth with people I did not know and letting Grandma King credit her side of the family for your eyes, your height, and the shape of your head. She needed you to belong to her—I understood.

You met your sister that day, a moment your father had been looking forward to, but not under those circumstances. She stared at you and her sad, dark eyes brightened when I placed you in her arms, and only hers.

"He looks like Daddy," she kept saying.

Your dad wanted so badly for you to know your sister and wrote in the journal that he hoped you would love and respect her. He talked about Christina often—her basketball playing, how pretty she was, funny stories of her childhood.

> *When your sister Christina was about three years old she was a busy little bee. I was stationed at Fort Hood, where I had guard duty at the air field. I got relieved early in the morning and brought home a case of chocolate milk. I put the case of milk in the refrigerator and went to sleep. I got up several hours later and went to the fridge to get chocolate milk. Well to my surprise Christina had pulled the wrappers off of each straw and inserted a straw in 24 milks. All I could do was laugh.*

Mostly because of his training schedule, but also because he divided his time off between Christina and me, your father did not see your sister as much as he would have liked after the divorce. He spent weeks with her in the summer and sent her gifts, from a telescope to new clothing, but he felt sad that he missed out on so much of her childhood.

*Your sister was born in Germany. She was born 29
August, 1990. Three months after she was born I was
deployed to Iraq. When I returned some six months
later she was already walking. I missed out on
watching her learn to walk.*

Christina left with us when I could not take a minute more of
having to wipe your hands and cheek with liquid sanitizer because
another great-aunt or wife of a cousin had kissed your fingers and
face. You were hungry and it was past your bedtime, I said.

Your sister wanted to feed you when we finally made it to our
room, and your father would have treasured that sight. You spit out
most of the strained carrots and apples, which was one of the only
times in those two days that I heard Christina laugh. I had met her
only once before, but she was family now and I wanted to soothe
her any way I could as the would-be stepmother of a hurting
sixteen-year-old.

"How are you doing?" I asked Christina, as she continued to
struggle with the carrots.

"Not too good," she answered with a shrug. She was her
daddy's daughter, pleasant and quiet, which made me worry. I
hoped she was opening up to her aunt and mother.

"You know that your daddy loved you very much," I said. "He
wanted so much to spend more time with you when he came
home. You will always be his first child."

Christina said she knew that—but her attention was still
on you.

"He has Daddy's head," she said, grinning.

As more family and friends arrived, surrounding us with so

much warmth, all I could think about was how alone and cold Charles must be in that steel box. I imagined it was lined with a plush fabric and remembered that he was wearing his army uniform. I tried to think of him as warm and comfortable. It is amazing the images your mind wants to hold on to when you are grieving.

I laid you next to me in bed instead of in the metal crib the hotel had provided—I just could not put you in that thing. You snuggled closer to me and I hummed to you as we fell asleep.

Storm clouds threatened the next morning, which of course would have made your father happy. Rain for the funeral, I thought, holding you at the window. God is in charge of Charles's homecoming.

I could not bring myself to dress you in black because your father would not have wanted that; you are our hope and promise and that part of him that lives on. You were so handsome as you looked at a swaying tree branch outside the window in your tiny navy blue pin-striped suit and tie.

I smoothed my black skirt and put on our coats. It was time to see your father off.

Charles's childhood church was already filled with mourners when we arrived—his beloved fifth-grade teacher, childhood friends, a woman who had a crush on him as a girl.

Selfishly, I wanted your father to myself one last time, but his family and friends had as much right as I did to bid him farewell— no one more so than his mother. I focused my irritation on the newspaper and television reporters at the back of the sanctuary, interlopers who did not even know my soldier. Then I remembered sitting in those same seats in so many churches as a journalist. It occurred to me for the first time how the families whose stories I had covered must have felt about me.

He would have been home in a month.

I tried to keep from shaking as I looked at the angel print on an easel next to Charles's casket, the same portrait that I had taken out of the closet and hung over your crib after he died. As unnerved as I had been when he gave it to me, it soothed me to see it beside him now. It was Charles's final way of doing what he had done so many times—comforting anyone who needed him.

As the organ's song began, my mind rewound to the first time I saw his smile, the first night we made love, the first time I laid you in his arms. I felt so alone in my grief, even surrounded by so many other heavy souls. Then I peered down the aisle and saw Charles's sister, Gail, sobbing and Christina's face streaked with tears as she rested in the curve of her mother's arm. Grandpa King seemed too tired even to breathe; his eyes were dry but his furrowed brow and twitching jaw hinted at his anguish. Your grandmother dabbed at her eyes as she stared somberly at the box now cradling her own baby.

Her fingernails were freshly painted magenta, which cheered me a little. Hard as losing her only son was, that hint of color suggested she was not about to succumb to her suffering. If a woman can manage to care about her fingernails in the midst of such pain, she is certainly not planning on giving up on life anytime soon.

Still, Charles would have been uncomfortable with so much grieving over him, and embarrassed by the spotlight on his character and accomplishments. Several mourners made mention of the page in the program that included his long list of military medals, fifty-six in all. They included two Bronze Stars, a Purple Heart, and eleven Army Achievement Medals.

I had never known about the honors, and Charles had never mentioned them to the rest of his family, either. I understood why.

There is no shame in taking pride in what you do. Just always remember to be humble. There is always someone who will be bigger and better than you, even if you do win the top trophy. Be thankful for all of your accomplishments.

It is true; if you don't use the talent God blessed you with it will fade away. But always share your gifts with others. That is how they will remember you, as the one who gives.

It was only by accident that we learned after your father died just how highly decorated he was. Gail and I were getting frustrated because his body had been at Dover for several days after he was flown out of Iraq, and she called the military to ask about the delay in releasing him for the funeral. They told her that it was a military funeral and they had to dress him, and that he had so many medals, some not stocked at Dover, that they had to wait for them all to arrive.

I was proud, just as I was during his funeral when a captain who had fought alongside him in Iraq and accompanied his body home eulogized him as a man who loved his soldiers and "would not let them do anything that he would not do."

The eulogies did not recount all the events that led to those medals, but many focused on First Sergeant King in combat and gave texture to the part of Charles's life that I knew least about— the part that he intentionally kept from me. In the beginning, he was simply too modest to talk about his heroism; later, he was too worried about upsetting me during my pregnancy to tell me much about his role in the army and the war.

Then the Reverend Vern Miller, Charles's childhood pastor, spoke, recalling the boy who helped with church chores, even bringing workers water all day when he was too little to lift heavy blocks for a parishioner's wall.

He concluded by sounding one small dissident note: "Chuckie came of age at a time when young people were supposed to believe that the government could be trusted. That was then. This is now."

When the color guard marched in to escort your father out of the church and I rose to stand, my legs almost buckled.

"No," I wanted to yell out. "Get away from him. I need him here with me. He has to stay; our baby needs him. God, let this be a dream. Please, please let me wake up."

But the pain was all too real and we had no choice but to follow your daddy to the cemetery as flakes of snow danced around us. I sat shivering under a green canopy with your sister and grandparents and shuddered with each shot of the three-volley salute during a military graveside service. A lone bugler played "Taps" in the distance.

The color guard lifted the flag off Charles's casket at the end of the ceremony and folded it with great precision into a tight triangle so that only the stars were visible. According to military tradition, once the triangle is presented, the flag and the soldier are retired. Charles's career had officially ended.

A soldier carried the flag as if it were a beating heart and walked slowly past me to Mr. and Mrs. King. He bent on one knee and presented the flag to them, saying, as per protocol, "This flag is presented on behalf of a grateful nation and the United States Army as a token of appreciation for your loved one's honorable and faithful service." Then he gave them a second one.

I was the "unofficial" widow and apparently not worthy of a flag or a letter of condolence from the president, or of the purple and gold lapel pin reserved for relatives of fallen soldiers, or of the set of your father's medals that he said he wanted you to have. Of course, I had no one to blame but myself—I had resisted marrying your father for so long. I had gambled that we would have a lifetime to be an official family. I was wrong.

Then I reminded myself that possessions weren't important—that he had already given me the thing he valued most.

I was haunted, too, by the fact that I had not been able to honor your father's wish to be buried in Arlington. When the time came to plan Charles's burial, the Kings chose this quiet spot near pine trees in a cemetery near his childhood home. Your grandmother said she needed Charles near so she could visit him, and it was clear that the matter was not open for debate. The Kings plan to be buried beside your dad when their time comes. I understand their decision, but I am just so sad for me and your father. How will we find our way back to each other if we are not buried together? Will Charles look for me? I know my soul will search for his.

My mother put her arm on my back to steady me. You were awake by then and sat still in my arms, bundled in your coat and a blanket. It was as though you understood the magnitude of the moment and wanted to do your father proud.

People began to walk back to their cars and I wondered how I would ever pull myself away from Charles's side. I carried you to your father's casket and placed your hand on it. Then I gave you to my mother and bent down to kiss the steel coffin, colder against my lips than it had been in the funeral parlor. It was time to go, but I just could not move. Then I felt my mother's hand on my back again. I saw you wiggling in her arms to stay warm and could almost hear your father order me to get you out of the cold. It was that voice—and it was you—that finally gave me the strength to push myself away.

It took several weeks back home, but we settled once again into

something of a routine—story time in the morning, your nap at noon, bath time at 6 p.m., a bedtime story. Then I would cry myself to sleep or clutch my belly in despair, wishing your father and I had planted another new life there before he left.

Then your grandmother King called about a memorial service for your father and his comrades at Fort Hood, in Killeen, Texas. I did not think I had the strength to go, but I knew your father would want his soldiers to meet his son.

Fort Hood had endured an alarming number of military casualties that October, twenty-one in all, and the memorial would pay tribute to all the fallen men.

When we arrived in Killeen, you awoke as we made our way from the open-air tarmac onto a bus and were hit by the chill of the evening air. Then, suddenly, it seemed as if the universe were playing a cruel joke. We were surrounded by groups of cheerful travelers—military families bubbling in anticipation of being reunited with loved ones returning from Iraq. There was a father in blue jeans clutching a "Welcome Home" sign, a wife applying fresh lipstick. I let them all get off the bus ahead of us.

At the end of a corridor leading to the concourse, a crowd of mothers, fathers, wives, lovers, and brothers and sisters waved American flags and broke into cheers and squeals when they spotted their hero. People collapsed in each other's arms, crying. I cried, too, happy tears for them and sad ones for *our* hero.

An officer met us in the concourse with Donna Morris, the soldier's wife who had been my "battle buddy." She wrapped her strong arms around us and I began to cry harder. I was releasing the pain of walking past those people with their signs and their soldiers, the pain of a reunion that would never be.

Donna took you out of my arms and smothered you in her warmth.

"My God, he looks just like the first sergeant," Donna said.

Finally, something to smile about.

Unfortunately, our bags were lost. After an hour of fruitless waiting, the officer said he would retrieve them later and took us to the Fisher House—a glorious place of comfort and healing. Until then I had never heard of the Fisher Foundation, a charitable organization that makes it possible for relatives of injured soldiers to stay nearby during a hospitalization. In this case, the Fisher House was reserved for the families attending the memorial.

Our bags had still not arrived the next morning and I was out of diapers and baby food, so I went into the communal kitchen to see if I could find any applesauce for you. A woman in a flower-print dress with sad eyes was sipping coffee. I drifted into the dining room, where a middle-aged couple holding hands nodded hello. A few other people milled about and began tentative conversations, first about who wanted bacon or needed their coffee warmed. But it did not take long for the awkward chatter to fall away. Soon a wholesome-looking woman with shaky hands was passing around pictures of her beloved boy smiling at his high school graduation a couple of years earlier. I sat beside her and let her talk. Her boy was kind, was transformed into a man by the army—and died more than six thousand miles from home.

I went back into the kitchen, where I was greeted by a man with one of the kindest faces I had ever seen. Isaac Howard was the caretaker of the Fisher House families. He was a black man well past middle age who spoke with a southern accent and wore a brimmed straw hat that he tipped when he said hello. Mr. Howard noticed me looking through the pantry and stepped toward me with a pen and paper.

"Write down what you need," he said.

"Well, I'm out of diapers but my son only eats organic baby

food. I'll just wait for it to arrive with my bags. I don't want you to go to any trouble searching for it."

"Ma'am, just write down what you need."

I smiled and thanked him and, sure enough, he returned within the hour with what I had asked for.

I was preparing your breakfast and watching you crawl around on the hardwood floor. Russ, a man who had lost his son and seemed to be barely holding up, walked slowly into the dining room. You were instantly drawn to him. Suddenly, you were crawling in his direction as fast as your legs could take you. You grabbed hold of his pants leg and lifted yourself into a standing position, reaching up for him. Somehow you sensed his need.

Russ swept you up in his arms and held you against his face and chest. He closed his eyes as he rocked with you, and you calmly patted his face. I was stunned. Russ dabbed at tears. He remembered when his son was that small, he said, and hugged you some more.

Moments like that were what Fisher House was about. It was a place where people in the most excruciating pain gathered with strangers who shared a similar grief. Heavy hearts were made lighter and miracles happened. We had just witnessed one.

The families of those dead soldiers smiled as they watched you crawl, playing with a green toy garbage truck that made burping noises. A woman asked if she could hold you and I said, "Of course." People passed more pictures around, told stories over tea.

The atmosphere became more somber by early afternoon; we all retreated to our rooms to start dressing for the ceremony. Soon everyone gathered in the living room, straightening neckties and fussing over hair and makeup, anxious distractions as we waited for the military vans. Most of the conversations stopped. One man was upset that he had forgotten a pin that he meant to wear on his lapel to honor his brother. His parents tried to calm him down.

The Kings were dignified and quiet, as always, standing erect in the foyer, following you with their eyes.

Then we stepped out of the safety of our cocoon and into the vans, the sun beaming down on all the suddenly lost souls, oblivious to our grief.

The army assigned a soldier to escort each family to its pew, but I was somehow left behind and walked in alone at the rear of the procession, carrying you in my arms. I tried to focus on what mattered. We were there to honor Charles even if such ceremonies were more for the living.

Christina was already seated with her mother and relatives when we walked in and took our seats in the row in front of theirs. Her face lit up when she saw you.

"You want to hold your baby brother, don't you?" I said.

She nodded excitedly and held out her arms, and so you snuggled with her until you became fussy. I wondered whether I should ask Christina if she wanted to move up and take her place with the King family, but I decided it was best not to make an issue of who walked in when and sat where.

Some families were already weeping. I somehow managed to maintain my composure, until an officer began barking out a ceremonial roll call of the dead soldiers' names. I knew what was coming and tried to brace myself.

"First Sergeant Charles Monroe King," the officer shouted. And then he let the silence linger where your father's response—"Sir, yes sir"—should have been.

I shook and sobbed uncontrollably, aching. I looked at you and wondered how we would ever carry on.

"He needs his daddy," I moaned to Charles's sister as she put her arm around me. "What am I going to do? He needs his daddy."

Her boyfriend lifted you out of my arms as I tried to compose myself. Who was going to teach you to be a man? I wondered as you played with his tie. Who would ever understand me the way Charles did? No one else would look at me with such passion—whether I had gained or lost weight, cut my hair or grown it long, had bad breath or a minty-fresh mouth. No one else would know my secrets, would kiss me like him, smell like he did.

It had taken a long time to find a love so powerful, and longer still to appreciate what I had found. I was certain it was as rare as a rainbow after a snowstorm and that I would never know it again.

The ceremony ended with "Taps." I wanted to leave, but so many people wanted to meet you. A slight white woman who appeared to be in her thirties approached me in the parking lot.

"Hi, I'm Valerie Lauer," she said. "I just want you to know that my husband told me that the first sergeant was the best boss he ever worked for. He really respected him."

I hugged and thanked her. She held me in her embrace longer than usual.

It was not until after she walked away that I realized who she was: her husband had died in the vehicle with your father. My eyes darted around the parking lot, searching for her. I did not find her again that day and felt sick that I had not offered condolences of my own.

When we finally made it back to the Fisher House, some of the families had already checked out and others were in their suites. You were the bright spirit that your grandparents, Christina, and I needed that evening. We had the living room to ourselves and laughed at your wobbly attempts at walking and fascination with some fake flowers in the room. Gail wanted to go through the belongings your father had left in storage near the base, but I did not want to leave you, and my grief was still so raw that I simply could not go through his things. She went without me.

We slept hard that night, you curled up next to me, both of us worn out from the long day. The morning came quickly and I said good-bye to the people with whom we had shared so much. I knew we would probably never see any of them again, just as I knew I would never forget their faces.

The public mourning was over, but the private pain was just beginning. It was there later, in New York, when I wrote *deceased* in the space intended for a father's name on the application for your preschool. It was there when I dreamed about Charles cradling my hips and awoke reaching for him. It was there when a cabdriver asked if I was married and I said no. It was always there.

Seventeen

Dear Jordan,

Saturday mornings are the hardest.

It is late fall 2007, barely a year since your dad died. I take you to the park before your afternoon nap and there are weeks when I am the only mother there. It took me a while to figure out why. It is daddy day. The mothers, I assume, are still sleeping, or reading the newspaper. Perhaps having lattes. I look out of place among the fathers chasing wobbly toddlers, or maybe I just feel that way.

There is nothing I would rather do on those mornings than watch you chase a bird or crunch leaves in your hands, but that weekly reminder of your father's absence can be wrenching. Once I sobbed so hard pushing you on a swing that I startled you. I did not hide my sorrow because in time you will understand that tears cleanse the soul like rain does the soil.

When the time is right, I will tell you the reason for my suffering. And I will show you the myriad ways in which your father is remembered—from the army training base in the Mojave Desert that was renamed FOB King after his death, to the quilt two strangers handmade for you in his honor.

For now, all I want for you is a typical childhood. So far our world revolves around playgroups, bubble baths, and endless readings of *Wheels on the Bus*. I rise when you do at 6 a.m., even though your dad used to tease that watching me wake up was like watching a baby suck a lemon.

The holidays can be cruel, though not even our first Father's Day was as torturous as the first winter after your father's death. That would have been our first holiday season as a family. On Thanksgiving, Charles would have held my hand and prayed over the Cornish hen and candied yams. He would have told God how much we had to be thankful for in the past year. On Christmas Day, he would have taken us to Central Park, just as he had promised. When we returned home, I would have put on holiday music and made hot apple cider.

Even in the depth of my grief over what we would have done and now would never be, I could not ignore your first Christmas. So on Christmas morning in 2006, just two months after your dad died, I watched you play with the wrapping paper and bows and pay little attention to the music box and stuffed animals. Then I zipped you in a fleece snowsuit and took you to Central Park alone. In a horse-drawn carriage, you and I snuggled under a blanket while the driver pointed out landmarks and I tried to smile. I could not keep it up. The driver seemed confused about why I was riding alone with a baby and weeping on Christmas Day. I told him.

When he helped me to the ground at the end of the trail, he said, "No charge." In a city that has a way of magnifying loneliness, it was an act of kindness I will never forget.

A few months ago, when you were about a year and a half, you started pointing to pictures of your father and saying "Daddy." I felt a rush of excitement the first time you said it, but then sadness. I was just so sorry that your father would never hear you say that beautiful word. Mostly, I was sad for you—that you will never again fall asleep in his arms, never feel his hand on your back on a park swing, never watch him shave.

And yet because of the journal he left, you will know your dad more intimately than many people know fathers who are living. Your father wrote a letter to you on the last page of the journal that I hope you will treasure as I do.

> *Dear Son,*
>
> *I hope this book is somewhat helpful to you. Please forgive me for the poor handwriting and grammar. I tried to finish this book before I was deployed to Iraq. It has to be something special to you. I've been writing in it in the states, Kuwait, and Iraq.*
>
> *I will do my best to make you and your mother proud of me. I will always be proud of you, my son.*
>
> *Be strong, take care of your family, and live life well. I love you and I love your mother. God Bless.*
>
> *Your Father,*
> *Charles King*

I also hope that what I have written will help you to understand the remarkable love your father and I shared. I want you to have that kind of love, Jordan. It is not the kind that always looks perfect. It is not the kind in which you promise never to go to bed mad. We sometimes did. No, it is more consequential than that.

It is the kind that will enable you to imagine loving a woman's wrinkled face someday, not simply the one that glows on your wedding day. It is a love that does not ask her to be anyone other than who she is, and that does not ask any more of you.

It also requires you to go on with your life if hers is cut short. You will talk, scream—or write—your way through the pain, because she would have expected no less.

It is not easy to teach all this by example. Grieving is a process you survive one heartbeat at a time, but finding the fortitude to endure is one of life's true wonders.

Before Charles was taken from me, I had never experienced death, except as a reporter covering a story. I always assumed I would be angry at God if someone close to me died. Just the opposite happened. There were days when my memories and prayers were all that got me through. Others were brightened by the most unexpected things. A box of herbal teas arrived with a note from a friend I had not heard from in years. A woman I worked with in Cleveland more than a decade ago sent us a collection of carols to help us through the holidays. A stay-at-home mother who lives in our building slipped a note under our door offering to sit with you if I needed a hand. Strangers who read about our loss sent cards and books and stuffed animals. A group of high school students from Connecticut wrote you letters that I am saving in a special box. The Art Institute of Chicago awarded your father an art degree posthumously.

The pain of losing the man I love still permeates my entire being, but so much munificence has been a salve. That is not to say I am the woman I used to be, the one who squealed at sunsets and danced barefoot in the living room. Because of your father's devotion, though, I am no longer the woman who did not believe in everlasting love.

Perhaps much further along in my healing I will find someone's hand to hold again. It is just too soon to imagine it. A boyfriend from college was in town recently and asked me out to dinner, and I accepted at the urging of family and friends. He had heard about your father's death but had probably not intended to spend the entire evening listening to me talk about him. My old friend was gracious—but he also wanted to know what I was doing to reclaim the feisty, vivacious woman he had known. I said that she was still deep within, but that I was not ready to think of myself as anything other than Charles's widow.

I will never be the same person I was, but I will be whole again, in time. What I pray for most is to be the kind of mother Charles deserved for his only son.

My prayer for you, Jordan, is that you carry with you the knowledge that you will always have two parents guiding you through life. I will rely on a mother's intuition to show you the way, but that alone will not be enough to teach you to be a man. For that, I give you your father's journal, and the wisdom it contains:

I will do my best to be the best example of a strong black man, physically, mentally, and spiritually.

Mission accomplished.

Epilogue

Dear Charles,

As I write this, it is January 2008, a year and three months since you went away. Our son is twenty-one months old and his energy is so infectious that it sustains us both when I am most weary. So does my certainty that you can hear me when I need to talk to you—not my voice, but the essence of what I have to say. This is what I need you to know:

You do not need to worry about Jordan and me. He is flourishing and I am finding my way, taking baby steps to regain my balance, just as Jordan did when he began to walk. I took a leave of absence from work to write because I needed so desperately to find an outlet for my grief. Writing has always been my salvation, as you know, and it has helped me to preserve your memory and our love.

There are still days when I cannot summon the strength even to brush my teeth. I have gained twenty-five pounds. I no longer bother putting on makeup or skirts or the leopard-print pumps you liked so much. A friend recently treated me to a tube of plum lipstick, trying to put some color back in my life, but I have yet to wear it. I sleep holding on to your favorite shirt when I am most lonely and sad—the faded blue-gray jersey you used to wear with jeans. Some nights, I roll it up and lay it across my chest so that it feels like your arm is still wrapped around me.

Then there are days when Jordan says a new word or looks at me with chocolate pudding on his nose and I hear myself laughing out loud. It is in those moments that I remember that life does go on.

I am not the only one coming to terms with that painful reality. Nearly one thousand more American soldiers have died in Iraq in the year since you were taken from us, and I grieve for the fathers and daughters and lovers who are feeling their way through the same darkness that I am. I pray that someone finds a way to end the fighting before another woman has to bury her man and another little boy is left with only photographs of his father to kiss.

Some of your soldiers are heading back for another tour of duty soon. I know that your spirit will be guiding them through. Others are still struggling to regain their lives. Your friend Tony retired early, just shy of twenty years of service, even though he once shared your dream of making sergeant major. He was so enraged by your death that he no longer wanted to wear the uniform. William Record is still receiving skin grafts and other medical treatment for his wounds, and as yet has no memory of the explosion. Jason Imhoff is still in the military. He continues to blame himself for what happened to you and calls me regularly.

In fact, you would be so proud to know how many of your men still call and visit us. Jordan has so many new uncles who want to tell him about you. It is amusing to watch their reaction when they see him for the first time. They draw a quick breath, stunned.

"My God, he looks just like the first sergeant," they inevitably say.

Jordan lost all his baby fat after he started walking and has been a mirror image of you ever since. Christina stares at him and shakes her head in amazement, too.

Your daughter is doing well, considering. She is about to graduate from high school and plans to spend part of the summer with us. I love telling her funny stories about your slow driving or the time you fought against going to a spa with me, then fell into a blissful sleep during the his-and-hers massages.

Being with her baby brother seems to comfort Christina. She dotes on Jordan when she visits, feeding him ice cream and chasing him around the children's museum. I am so sorry you never got to see them together, just as I am that you never got to see what a spirited, confident boy your son has become.

Our son has already learned to climb out of the crib we bought when I was pregnant. I replaced it with a "big boy bed" that one of my girlfriends helped me put together. He has not actually slept an entire night there, though, because he prefers your spot in our bed. (We're working on it.)

Jordan has become quite the little New Yorker, too. He already knows how to hail a taxi and recently sat through an entire play at a children's theater in Greenwich Village.

It is too early to tell how your death will affect him or how much he misses you, though I know that he does. Some days he covers his eyes and says "peek-a-boo, Daddy." I sobbed the first time he did it but now his little game makes me smile. I wonder if you are actually there playing with him.

Like me, Jordan's favorite question is "Why?" The answers are simple for now: because the oven is hot, because eating that plastic could cause you to choke. One day he will ask "Why?" and there will be no easy answers. When that time comes, I will be honest. If he wants to know what this war was about and what I thought of it, I will tell him.

All I have said so far is that his daddy is a hero who wrote a beautiful journal for him. I said that you made sure that all of our needs would be taken care of if you were called on to make the ultimate sacrifice. I said you were just that kind of man.

I know he did not understand all of what I said, but I will keep telling him until he does. He should know that Mommy will always take care of him, but that I am not doing it alone.

I am also trying to find ways to take care of myself. You remember the spot on my ankle that you liked to kiss? I have had your name tattooed there, a permanent symbol of our love and a substitute for the wedding band I will never wear. As the artist carved the thin script into my skin and surrounded it with tiny hearts and delicate swirls, I welcomed the sting of the needle, distracting me from the larger pain.

A friend gently asked if I had considered what another man might someday think of the tattoo. I said that I would hope he would understand that it is the mark of a woman whose love is forever. But the truth is I cannot imagine falling in love again.

I would trade a lifetime with anyone else for just one more day with you. I would tell you I am haunted by guilt for the years I wasted questioning whether we were right for each other. I would tell you that you taught me how to love, and that you helped me to be a better woman because of the dignity with which you lived your life. I would savor your smile as you watched our little boy play and would let my fingers trace the lines of your face and the veins on your hands.

Then I would put Jordan in your arms one last time and lie there with him until you had to go home again.

It has been hard accepting that I am a widow, but I know the time has come to start focusing on my future without you. It is time for me to get back in the gym, which would no doubt amuse you. I may take Jordan to visit friends in Paris in the spring. I might even put on that plum lipstick someday soon and go to a jazz club with my girlfriends.

I know that the more I heal the easier you will rest, and the more present I will be as a mother. Mostly, though, I owe it to myself to find a reason to dance again.

Jordan and I were cuddling in bed the other morning and he touched my face and said, "I happy."

I held him tighter, drawing on his warmth and his exuberance.

"I'm happy, too," I said.

At that moment, at least, I meant it.

Author's Note

The thing that has guided me most in writing this memoir is the knowledge that the ultimate reader of it is my son, Jordan.

All of the people and events in this book are real. The chronology is as exact as I remember it. Memory is imperfect, but all the dialogue between Charles and me is also exactly as I remember it, with no embellishments. Where I have quoted my family, Charles's family, the soldiers who served with Charles, or other military personnel, those quotations are drawn from interviews conducted by me or, in some cases, one of my two research assistants.

The majority of the extracts from Charles's journal are exactly as he wrote them. In two or three instances, I've combined similar entries. I have also made very minor changes to spelling, grammar, and punctuation for the sake of clarity.

I am mindful of the fact that I have written about some extremely personal matters related to both my family and to Charles's family. I have included only those details I believe to be essential if Jordan and the reader are to understand Charles and me and how our relationship unfolded. I hope our families will forgive me any errors, and that they will understand the spirit in which the book is written and my desire to tell Jordan the truth about his parents' lives.

Acknowledgments

There are so many people I must thank for being a part of this book, whether through inspiration or direct involvement.

Foremost, to Almighty God, I humbly thank you for the gift of Charles and Jordan. I thank you, too, for blessing me with a talent and passion for writing. Above all, I thank you for your everlasting love. I seek to be in service to you with this book and in all that I do.

There are no words sufficient to express my gratitude to the men who served with my Charles in the 1st Battalion, 67th Armored Regiment, 2nd Brigade, 4th Infantry Division from Fort Hood, Texas—the Dealers. Charles loved each and every one of you! Thank you especially to all of the Dealers who spent hours letting me interview you for this book. I will never forget you or your generosity.

To Tony Jenkins, Charles could not have had a better battle buddy. Thank you for being there for him, and now for Jordan and me. Charles also could not have chosen a better battle buddy for me than he did in Donna Morris. You have been my rock, Donna, both when our men were in Iraq and since we lost Charles. Thank you for putting me in touch with so many Dealers to research this book and for letting me call on you and Kenny so often in the crafting of it. Your giving spirit is one of the reasons Charles loved you, as do I.

Acknowledgments

To Valerie Lauer, with whom I share an unspoken bond, both having lost the men we loved that dreadful October day, thank you for reaching out to me in so many ways, and for sharing your memories with me. And to William Record and the family of Joseph Kane, I never had the honor of meeting you, but I share in your pain and am sorry for your suffering. Know that I continue to pray for you.

To all of the men and women of the United States Armed Forces, I thank you for your service and your sacrifices. You inspire me. Godspeed to you and your families.

To Mr. Charlie King and Mrs. Gladys King, your son would not have been the amazing man he was without you as his parents. I thank you for his life, and I want you to know that I will love him for the rest of mine. To Christina, thank you for sharing your daddy with me, and for being such a loving "sissy" to Jordan. We love you dearly. To Gail, for all that you meant to your brother.

To my father, Thomas J. Canedy Sr., and to my mother, Penny Canedy, thank you for your enduring love and for supporting me every step of the way in writing this book. For as long as I can remember, you have encouraged me to write, even when I was a young girl penning poems about autumn leaves.

To my devoted brothers and sisters: David, Lynnette, Thomas Jr., Kim, Nikki, Vanessa, and Derrick, you are my best friends and I love you with all of my heart. To my precious nieces and nephews: Michael, Mariah, Aaliyah, Imani, Kayla, Brianna, Alana, Cameron, Collin, Brian, and Dominic, Aunt Dana adores you.

To Grandma Everlener Canedy and Aunt Bobbie Williams, you are always in my heart.

To Rachel Klayman, my editor at Crown, words fail me in describing your extraordinary talent. I am in awe of how much your deft editing improved my manuscript, and of how passionately you cared about my story. I have often told you that, second only to giving birth to Jordan, this is the most important endeavor of my life. I would not have wanted to undertake it with anyone else. You laughed with me, cried with me, and counseled me as we made it through the emotionally wrenching chapters. I thank you for all that you did to make the story come to life, and I know that Charles does, too.

I am so grateful that my book landed at Crown. It found a home there that is warm and safe and nurturing. To Jenny Frost, thank you for giving me the time, the space, and the support to tell my story. To Tina Constable, who is an author's publisher, that is to say supportive in every conceivable way, I have grown to respect you for so many things, especially your boundless enthusiasm. To Philip Patrick, you did me the great honor of making me feel as though this project was personal to you. To Tara Gilbride, Cindy Berman, and Mary Choteborsky, for your amazing talent and support, and to Mary Anne Stewart, for your sensitivity and incredibly thorough copyediting. Thanks to everyone else at Crown who helped make this book a reality.

To my agent, Flip Brophy, my biggest cheerleader for this book, your professionalism and your wit are matched only by your enormous heart. You were with me all along, especially when the pain of losing Charles was so overwhelming. I remember standing on a street corner crying my eyes out one day, and how you were there beside me with outstretched arms to ease my pain. That was not in your job description but says so much about who you are. Thank you.

To Sharon Skettini, Flip's assistant, you are a talented young woman who I have no doubt will someday be running the place. To everyone else at Sterling Lord Literistic, you are the best team in the business. Thanks to you all for your unwavering enthusiasm.

To Rebecca Corbett, my "official reader," colleague, and friend, I thank you so very much for guiding me through the writing of this book, for reading each draft of every chapter, and lending me your considerable skills and wisdom as I sat down to what was initially just an idea and a blank computer screen. I might still be staring at an empty page if not for you.

To Miriam Hill, my oldest friend, can you believe it's been more than twenty years? Here's to many more decades of girl talk, laughter, and love. Thank you for being by my side when Jordan was born and for encouraging me to write this book.

To my sistah soul mates: Rachel Swarns, Robin Stone, Katti Gray, and Cynthia Curry, we are family, you know that. Thanks for reading early drafts of some chapters, helping me to remember details of my time with Charles, and for always having my back. I've got yours, too.

To my girls: Mia Navarro, Becky Carusso, Jennifer Preston, Janet Elder, Loretta James, and Jahovanny Espinal, I am a richer, happier person for knowing each of you. Thank you especially to Jahovanny, for babysitting when I was on deadline for this book.

To Lilian Polanco, Charles and I could not have asked for a more compassionate person to care for our son. Your love for Jordan, and his for you, enabled me to focus on reporting and writing without worrying about his welfare. You are doing God's work.

To Dorothy Cunningham, you are one special dame. Thank you for talking me through the telling of my story.

To Major Nathan Banks, thank you for giving so generously of your time and knowledge while I was researching the military information for my book. I appreciate your patience and attention to detail. I am in your debt.

To my talented research assistants, Terry Aguayo and Lilliana Polanco, thank you for all of your hard work, especially the painstaking fact-checking. I know I required a lot of you, but I never doubted you would come through. I owe you both.

I want to thank my colleagues at the *New York Times* for helping me cope with Charles's death and for being the first ones to show an interest in our story. I still remember coming back to work after he died and finding flowers and teddy bears on my desk and a mailbox stuffed with cards. I am grateful, too, for the scholarship fund for Jordan to which so many of you have contributed. I especially want to thank Jill Abramson, my boss and friend. You were the first one who saw the potential for this book and encouraged me to write it. You walked with me in the park when I was feeling alone and lost. You even went shoe shopping with me when I needed a pick-me-up. What more could a girl ask for? I am so grateful for your friendship. Thank you, too, to Bill Schmidt and Glenn Kramon. I don't think you realize how much your presence at Charles's funeral helped me through that day, or how much of a difference your support since then has made.

To Kathleen McElroy and Grace Wong, thank you so much for being there in so many ways to help me through the toughest time of my life.

To Karen Kantor and Stanley Tobin and to Shawn Rogers, thank you for your amazing friendship, for supporting my book, and for helping me to "punch" my way through this time in my life. Let's keep the gloves up.

To Roz Lichter, this book would never have been written without you. Thanks for all that you did to make it possible. Thank you also to Shaika Roberts for helping me to maintain an orderly home at a time when my sole focus was on my two babies—Jordan and this book.

I also want to humbly thank every reader of this book. I never intended to put my life on public display, but Charles and I shared a rare love and, after his death, I simply had to share our story and his spirit. My best to every one of you.

About the Author

DANA CANEDY is the executive vice president and publisher of Simon & Schuster. Previously, she was the administrator of the Pulitzer Prizes and a senior editor at the *New York Times,* where she was a journalist for twenty years. In 2001, Dana was part of a team at the *New York Times* that won a Pulitzer Prize for national reporting for "How Race Is Lived in America," a series on race relations in the United States. She served as the paper's Florida bureau chief during the 2000 presidential recount and the Columbia space shuttle explosion in 2003. She has also been assistant editor for national news at the *New York Times,* responsible for overseeing breaking national news coverage, and a business and finance reporter.

Before joining the *New York Times,* Dana was a reporter at the *Plain Dealer* in Cleveland and the *Palm Beach Post* in West Palm Beach, Florida. She graduated from the University of Kentucky with a bachelor's degree in journalism. Dana lives in New York City.

Reading Group Guide

1. When Dana describes her ideal man, she envisions someone like her New York self. Should an ideal mate be like you or unlike you? How does her ideal evolve?

2. How are Dana and Charles different and how are they similar? Are they as different as Dana thinks?

3. How does Dana's ambivalence toward her father affect her relationship with men? How does her view of her father change after Jordan is born? If you have children, did parenthood make you more or less accepting of your parents?

4. How do Charles' and Dana's experiences as African Americans shape their choices?

5. Both Dana and Charles struggle to balance challenging careers and their personal lives. How have you dealt with those demands in your life? What factors led Dana to shift her priorities and decide to have a child just as Charles was about to be deployed to Iraq?

6. The book captures both the fast-paced world of journalism and the rigors of military life. What did you find interesting or surprising about their vocations?

7. How did the chapters on Iraq affect you? Did it deepen your understanding of what is asked of soldiers and the nature of this war?

8. When Charles tells Dana that he will miss Jordan's birth because his soldiers need him, do you understand his decision?

9. Discuss the role of religious faith for Charles. How does Dana interpret his angel portrait? What does the drawing mean to Charles?

10. When Dana investigates the fatal mission, she discovers that the military often sanitizes the circumstances of a soldier's death. Should loved ones be protected from the truth in this way?

11. Dana learns things she didn't know about Charles from his journal. Do we ever fully know the ones we love? Does this book inspire you to learn more about your loved ones?

12. Dana depicts a mature, romantic love. How do you feel about her decision to present their relationship, flaws and all, to their son? How is love defined? What does Dana mean when she says, "I realized that day our relationship would never be perfect. Only perfect for us"?

13. Why does Dana make each chapter a letter? How does she use Charles' journal and to what effect? What makes this book a compelling read that transcends one family's grief?

14. What is a father? Does anything in *A Journal for Jordan* lead you to rethink your definition?